Be careful!!

This planner belongs to an author.

Please call

_____

if found.

You've been
warned.

My Speculative Daily Planner
2019

_____

Name

_____

Email

Crystal Lake Publishing
www.CrystalLakePub.com

Awesome Author Signatures:

_____

_____   _____
Printed Name   Date

_____

_____   _____
Printed Name   Date

_____

_____   _____
Printed Name   Date

_____

_____   _____
Printed Name   Date

Awesome Author Signatures:

_____

_____   _____

Printed Name   Date

_____

_____   _____

Printed Name   Date

_____

_____   _____

Printed Name   Date

_____

_____   _____

Printed Name   Date

What's happening where and when this year?

(This is not a complete list of all conventions happening in 2019. Please be advised that the schedules of many of these is tentative and subject to change)

MystiCon: February 22-24, Roanoke, Virginia

Con-Tagion: February 9, Charlotte, North Carolina

Mad Monster Party: February 22-24, Charlotte, North Carolina

Midsouth Con: March 15-17, Memphis, Tennessee

Spooky Empire: March 22-24, Orlando, Florida

RavenCon: April 5-7, Williamsburg, Virginia

Texas Frightmare Weekend: May 3-5, Dallas, Texas

Necon: July 19-21, Pawtucket, Rhode Island

Scares That Care Weekend: August 2-4, Williamsburg, Virginia

Killercon: Aug 16-18, Wingate by Wyndham Round Rock, Texas

NecronomiCon: August 22-25, Providence, Rhode Island

Women in Horror Film Festival: Oct. 4-7, Atlanta, Georgia

Bouchercon: Oct 31-Nov 3, Dallas, Texas

My Contacts:

Name	number	email
_____	_____	_____
_____	_____	_____
_____	_____	_____
_____	_____	_____
_____	_____	_____
_____	_____	_____
_____	_____	_____
_____	_____	_____
_____	_____	_____
_____	_____	_____
_____	_____	_____
_____	_____	_____
_____	_____	_____
_____	_____	_____

"Nobody tells this to people who are beginners, I wish someone told me. All of us who do creative work, we get into it because we have good taste. But there is this gap. For the first couple years you make stuff, it's just not that good. It's trying to be good, it has potential, but it's not. But your taste, the thing that got you into the game, is still killer. And your taste is why your work disappoints you. A lot of people never get past this phase, they quit. Most people I know who do interesting, creative work went through years of this. We know our work doesn't have this special thing that we want it to have. We all go through this. And if you are just starting out or you are still in this phase, you gotta know its normal and the most important thing you can do is do a lot of work. Put yourself on a deadline so that every week you will finish one story. It is only by going through a volume of work that you will close that gap, and your work will be as good as your ambitions. And I took longer to figure out how to do this than anyone I've ever met. It's gonna take awhile. It's normal to take awhile. You've just gotta fight your way through."

—Ira Glass

UNIVERSITY OF RICHARD

Email Richard Thomas now for a course guide
writingwithrichard@gmail.com

BRAM STOKER, SHIRLEY JACKSON, AND THRILLER AWARD NOMINEE
AUTHOR OF SEVEN BOOKS AND 150 STORIES, EDITOR OF FOUR ANTHOLOGIES
EDITOR-IN-CHIEF OF DARK HOUSE PRESS AND GAMUT MAGAZINE

Short Story Mechanics • Contemporary Dark Fiction
Advanced Creative Writing Workshop
Keep it Brief: Flash Fiction • Novel in a Year

Weekly Planner

_____ to _____

Goals

_____

_____

_____

_____

_____

Notes

MONDAY _____

TUESDAY _____

WEDNESDAY _____

THURSDAY _____

FRIDAY _____

SATURDAY _____

SUNDAY _____

Monday

12/31/2018

Things to Accomplish

_____

_____

_____

_____

Writing Goals

_____

_____

_____

"The question isn't who is going to let me; It's who is going to stop me."—Ayn Rand

5:00 AM	
6:00 AM	
7:00 AM	
8:00 AM	
9:00 AM	
10:00 AM	
11:00 AM	
12:00 PM	
1:00 PM	
2:00 PM	
3:00 PM	
4:00 PM	
5:00 PM	
6:00 PM	
7:00 PM	
8:00 PM	
9:00 PM	
10:00 PM	
11:00 PM	

Tuesday

1/1/2019

Things to Accomplish

_____

_____

_____

_____

Writing Goals

_____

_____

_____

"When I stepped from hard manual work to writing, I just stepped from one kind of hard work to another."
—Sean O'Casey

5:00 AM	
6:00 AM	
7:00 AM	
8:00 AM	
9:00 AM	
10:00 AM	
11:00 AM	
12:00 PM	
1:00 PM	
2:00 PM	
3:00 PM	
4:00 PM	
5:00 PM	
6:00 PM	
7:00 PM	
8:00 PM	
9:00 PM	
10:00 PM	
11:00 PM	

Wednesday

1/2/2019

Things to Accomplish

_____

_____

_____

Writing Goals

_____

_____

_____

"For best results and not falling asleep in your chair, write 30 min. move 10 min. I use a kitchen timer in my shirt pocket."—Brian J. Lewis

5:00 AM	
6:00 AM	
7:00 AM	
8:00 AM	
9:00 AM	
10:00 AM	
11:00 AM	
12:00 PM	
1:00 PM	
2:00 PM	
3:00 PM	
4:00 PM	
5:00 PM	
6:00 PM	
7:00 PM	
8:00 PM	
9:00 PM	
10:00 PM	
11:00 PM	

Thursday

1/3/2019

Things to Accomplish

_____

_____

_____

_____

Writing Goals

_____

_____

_____

"Writing is utter solitude, the descent into the cold abyss of oneself."—Franz Kafka

5:00 AM	
6:00 AM	
7:00 AM	
8:00 AM	
9:00 AM	
10:00 AM	
11:00 AM	
12:00 PM	
1:00 PM	
2:00 PM	
3:00 PM	
4:00 PM	
5:00 PM	
6:00 PM	
7:00 PM	
8:00 PM	
9:00 PM	
10:00 PM	
11:00 PM	

Friday

1/4/2019

Things to Accomplish

_____

_____

_____

_____

Writing Goals

_____

_____

_____

"As a writer one is allowed to have conversations with oneself. What is considered sane in writers is mad for the rest of the human race."
—Alan Ayckbourn

5:00 AM	
6:00 AM	
7:00 AM	
8:00 AM	
9:00 AM	
10:00 AM	
11:00 AM	
12:00 PM	
1:00 PM	
2:00 PM	
3:00 PM	
4:00 PM	
5:00 PM	
6:00 PM	
7:00 PM	
8:00 PM	
9:00 PM	
10:00 PM	
11:00 PM	

Saturday

1/5/2019

Things to Accomplish

_____

_____

_____

_____

Writing Goals

_____

_____

_____

"Do the one thing today that
most reminds you why you
love your life."—Joe Mynhardt

5:00 AM	
6:00 AM	
7:00 AM	
8:00 AM	
9:00 AM	
10:00 AM	
11:00 AM	
12:00 PM	
1:00 PM	
2:00 PM	
3:00 PM	
4:00 PM	
5:00 PM	
6:00 PM	
7:00 PM	
8:00 PM	
9:00 PM	
10:00 PM	
11:00 PM	

Sunday

1/6/2019

Things to Accomplish

_____

_____

_____

_____

Writing Goals

_____

_____

_____

Watch 10-15 minutes of a movie, or an episode of a TV show and write it as prose. Try to get into the character's heads, describe the setting and what's happening. Obviously, you won't be able to use it for anything, but it will help in terms of visualising your own writing.—Paul Kane

5:00 AM	
6:00 AM	
7:00 AM	
8:00 AM	
9:00 AM	
10:00 AM	
11:00 AM	
12:00 PM	
1:00 PM	
2:00 PM	
3:00 PM	
4:00 PM	
5:00 PM	
6:00 PM	
7:00 PM	
8:00 PM	
9:00 PM	
10:00 PM	
11:00 PM	

Weekly Planner

_____ to _____

Goals

_____

_____

_____

_____

_____

Notes

MONDAY _____

TUESDAY _____

WEDNESDAY _____

THURSDAY _____

FRIDAY _____

SATURDAY _____

SUNDAY _____

Monday

1/7/2019

Things to Accomplish

_____

_____

_____

_____

Writing Goals

_____

_____

_____

"The only way to fail is to quit."—Ray Bradbury

5:00 AM	
6:00 AM	
7:00 AM	
8:00 AM	
9:00 AM	
10:00 AM	
11:00 AM	
12:00 PM	
1:00 PM	
2:00 PM	
3:00 PM	
4:00 PM	
5:00 PM	
6:00 PM	
7:00 PM	
8:00 PM	
9:00 PM	
10:00 PM	
11:00 PM	

Tuesday

1/8/2019

Things to Accomplish

_____

_____

_____

_____

Writing Goals

_____

_____

_____

"Don't let the reputation of gore and blood about Horror define your love for a genre that is smart, honest, and reflective. One that offers hope amid pages of terror, fear, and the unknown. Don't settle for cliché. Aim higher. Don't give up on Horror, writing, the readers, or yourselves."—Sheldon Higdon

5:00 AM	
6:00 AM	
7:00 AM	
8:00 AM	
9:00 AM	
10:00 AM	
11:00 AM	
12:00 PM	
1:00 PM	
2:00 PM	
3:00 PM	
4:00 PM	
5:00 PM	
6:00 PM	
7:00 PM	
8:00 PM	
9:00 PM	
10:00 PM	
11:00 PM	

Wednesday

1/9/2019

Things to Accomplish

_____

_____

_____

_____

Writing Goals

_____

_____

_____

"Writing means not just
staring ugliness in the face,
but finding a way to embrace
it."—Veronica Roth

5:00 AM	
6:00 AM	
7:00 AM	
8:00 AM	
9:00 AM	
10:00 AM	
11:00 AM	
12:00 PM	
1:00 PM	
2:00 PM	
3:00 PM	
4:00 PM	
5:00 PM	
6:00 PM	
7:00 PM	
8:00 PM	
9:00 PM	
10:00 PM	
11:00 PM	

Thursday

1/10/2019

Things to Accomplish

_____

_____

_____

_____

Writing Goals

_____

_____

_____

Make a list of your five favorite authors, books, genres, movies, and tv shows. Look for the similarities; look for the outliers. These are your influences, so this is probably your writing voice. What would you call it? After making my lists, I ended up calling my work neo-noir, speculative fiction with a literary bent. You?—Richard Thomas

5:00 AM	
6:00 AM	
7:00 AM	
8:00 AM	
9:00 AM	
10:00 AM	
11:00 AM	
12:00 PM	
1:00 PM	
2:00 PM	
3:00 PM	
4:00 PM	
5:00 PM	
6:00 PM	
7:00 PM	
8:00 PM	
9:00 PM	
10:00 PM	
11:00 PM	

Friday

1/11/2019

Things to Accomplish

_____

_____

_____

_____

Writing Goals

_____

_____

_____

"You're never alone when you're a writer. You have all those voices and characters in your head to keep you company!"—John Palisano

5:00 AM	
6:00 AM	
7:00 AM	
8:00 AM	
9:00 AM	
10:00 AM	
11:00 AM	
12:00 PM	
1:00 PM	
2:00 PM	
3:00 PM	
4:00 PM	
5:00 PM	
6:00 PM	
7:00 PM	
8:00 PM	
9:00 PM	
10:00 PM	
11:00 PM	

Saturday

1/12/2019

Things to Accomplish

_____

_____

_____

_____

Writing Goals

_____

_____

_____

"Some of my favorite short stories that I've written came straight from nightmares. Very little embellishment or change, just a straight up dictation of my psyche's sleeping projection of terror."—Mark Sheldon

5:00 AM	
6:00 AM	
7:00 AM	
8:00 AM	
9:00 AM	
10:00 AM	
11:00 AM	
12:00 PM	
1:00 PM	
2:00 PM	
3:00 PM	
4:00 PM	
5:00 PM	
6:00 PM	
7:00 PM	
8:00 PM	
9:00 PM	
10:00 PM	
11:00 PM	

Sunday

1/13/2019

Things to Accomplish

_____

_____

_____

_____

Writing Goals

_____

_____

_____

"Writing is the only thing that when I do it, I don't feel I should be doing something else."—Gloria Steinem

5:00 AM	
6:00 AM	
7:00 AM	
8:00 AM	
9:00 AM	
10:00 AM	
11:00 AM	
12:00 PM	
1:00 PM	
2:00 PM	
3:00 PM	
4:00 PM	
5:00 PM	
6:00 PM	
7:00 PM	
8:00 PM	
9:00 PM	
10:00 PM	
11:00 PM	

Weekly Planner

_____ to _____

Goals

_____

_____

_____

_____

Notes

MONDAY _____

TUESDAY _____

WEDNESDAY _____

THURSDAY _____

FRIDAY _____

SATURDAY _____

SUNDAY _____

Monday

1/14/2019

Things to Accomplish

_____

_____

_____

_____

Writing Goals

_____

_____

_____

"Whether you succeed or not is irrelevant, there is no such thing. Making your unknown known is the important thing."—Georgia O'Keeffe

5:00 AM	
6:00 AM	
7:00 AM	
8:00 AM	
9:00 AM	
10:00 AM	
11:00 AM	
12:00 PM	
1:00 PM	
2:00 PM	
3:00 PM	
4:00 PM	
5:00 PM	
6:00 PM	
7:00 PM	
8:00 PM	
9:00 PM	
10:00 PM	
11:00 PM	

Tuesday

1/15/2019

Things to Accomplish

_____

_____

_____

_____

Writing Goals

_____

_____

_____

"Don't think about making art, just get it done. Let everyone else decide if it's good or bad, whether they love it or hate it. While they are deciding, make even more art."—Andy Warhol

5:00 AM	
6:00 AM	
7:00 AM	
8:00 AM	
9:00 AM	
10:00 AM	
11:00 AM	
12:00 PM	
1:00 PM	
2:00 PM	
3:00 PM	
4:00 PM	
5:00 PM	
6:00 PM	
7:00 PM	
8:00 PM	
9:00 PM	
10:00 PM	
11:00 PM	

Wednesday

1/16/2019

Things to Accomplish

_____

_____

_____

_____

Writing Goals

_____

_____

_____

"I shut my eyes in order to see."—Paul Gauguin

5:00 AM	
6:00 AM	
7:00 AM	
8:00 AM	
9:00 AM	
10:00 AM	
11:00 AM	
12:00 PM	
1:00 PM	
2:00 PM	
3:00 PM	
4:00 PM	
5:00 PM	
6:00 PM	
7:00 PM	
8:00 PM	
9:00 PM	
10:00 PM	
11:00 PM	

Thursday

1/17/2019

Things to Accomplish

_____

_____

_____

_____

Writing Goals

_____

_____

_____

"Inspiration is for amateurs.
The rest of us just show up
and get to work."
—Chuck Close

5:00 AM	
6:00 AM	
7:00 AM	
8:00 AM	
9:00 AM	
10:00 AM	
11:00 AM	
12:00 PM	
1:00 PM	
2:00 PM	
3:00 PM	
4:00 PM	
5:00 PM	
6:00 PM	
7:00 PM	
8:00 PM	
9:00 PM	
10:00 PM	
11:00 PM	

Friday

1/18/2019

Things to Accomplish

_____

_____

_____

_____

Writing Goals

_____

_____

_____

Don't stall writing your book struggling for a knock out first chapter if inspiration doesn't come. Dive straight in to an exciting, powerful scene anywhere in the story. The rest will either form around it or it could become the start the book was crying out for.
—Raven Dane.

5:00 AM	
6:00 AM	
7:00 AM	
8:00 AM	
9:00 AM	
10:00 AM	
11:00 AM	
12:00 PM	
1:00 PM	
2:00 PM	
3:00 PM	
4:00 PM	
5:00 PM	
6:00 PM	
7:00 PM	
8:00 PM	
9:00 PM	
10:00 PM	
11:00 PM	

Saturday

1/19/2019

Things to Accomplish

_____

_____

_____

_____

Writing Goals

_____

_____

_____

"The scariest moment is always just before you start."— Stephen King

5:00 AM	
6:00 AM	
7:00 AM	
8:00 AM	
9:00 AM	
10:00 AM	
11:00 AM	
12:00 PM	
1:00 PM	
2:00 PM	
3:00 PM	
4:00 PM	
5:00 PM	
6:00 PM	
7:00 PM	
8:00 PM	
9:00 PM	
10:00 PM	
11:00 PM	

Sunday
1/20/2019

Things to Accomplish

_____

_____

_____

_____

Writing Goals

_____

_____

_____

"Don't say the old lady
screamed. Bring her on and
let her scream."—Mark Twain

5:00 AM	
6:00 AM	
7:00 AM	
8:00 AM	
9:00 AM	
10:00 AM	
11:00 AM	
12:00 PM	
1:00 PM	
2:00 PM	
3:00 PM	
4:00 PM	
5:00 PM	
6:00 PM	
7:00 PM	
8:00 PM	
9:00 PM	
10:00 PM	
11:00 PM	

Weekly Planner

_____ to _____

Goals

_____

_____

_____

_____

_____

Notes

MONDAY _____

TUESDAY _____

WEDNESDAY _____

THURSDAY _____

FRIDAY _____

SATURDAY _____

SUNDAY _____

Monday

1/21/2019

Things to Accomplish

_____

_____

_____

_____

Writing Goals

_____

_____

_____

"If you can tell stories, create characters, devise incidents, and have sincerity and passion, it doesn't matter a damn how you write."
—Somerset Maugham

5:00 AM	
6:00 AM	
7:00 AM	
8:00 AM	
9:00 AM	
10:00 AM	
11:00 AM	
12:00 PM	
1:00 PM	
2:00 PM	
3:00 PM	
4:00 PM	
5:00 PM	
6:00 PM	
7:00 PM	
8:00 PM	
9:00 PM	
10:00 PM	
11:00 PM	

Tuesday

1/22/2019

Things to Accomplish

_____

_____

_____

_____

Writing Goals

_____

_____

_____

"Be vulnerable. Readers crave a writer's scars, warts and all. The prospect of bearing too much can be daunting, sure, but that makes characters real, and readers remember that connection long after they put down your work. Don't be afraid to show your cards."—Matt Hayward

5:00 AM	
6:00 AM	
7:00 AM	
8:00 AM	
9:00 AM	
10:00 AM	
11:00 AM	
12:00 PM	
1:00 PM	
2:00 PM	
3:00 PM	
4:00 PM	
5:00 PM	
6:00 PM	
7:00 PM	
8:00 PM	
9:00 PM	
10:00 PM	
11:00 PM	

Wednesday

1/23/2019

Things to Accomplish

_____

_____

_____

_____

Writing Goals

_____

_____

_____

"Harness the power of the micro-session! Many of us have lives that are so busy it can be hard to find big blocks of writing time, which is why we need to train ourselves to write in minutes."—Lisa Morton

5:00 AM	
6:00 AM	
7:00 AM	
8:00 AM	
9:00 AM	
10:00 AM	
11:00 AM	
12:00 PM	
1:00 PM	
2:00 PM	
3:00 PM	
4:00 PM	
5:00 PM	
6:00 PM	
7:00 PM	
8:00 PM	
9:00 PM	
10:00 PM	
11:00 PM	

Thursday
1/24/2019

Things to Accomplish

_____

_____

_____

_____

Writing Goals

_____

_____

_____

"If you are not afraid of the
voices inside you, you will not
fear the critics outside you."
—Natalie Goldberg

5:00 AM	
6:00 AM	
7:00 AM	
8:00 AM	
9:00 AM	
10:00 AM	
11:00 AM	
12:00 PM	
1:00 PM	
2:00 PM	
3:00 PM	
4:00 PM	
5:00 PM	
6:00 PM	
7:00 PM	
8:00 PM	
9:00 PM	
10:00 PM	
11:00 PM	

Friday

1/25/2019

Things to Accomplish

_____

_____

_____

_____

Writing Goals

_____

_____

_____

You see a weather beaten picnic table, set alone in the centre of a clearing. Thick forest surrounds on all sides. On the table is a hat, weighted with stones. Write the story of how the hat ended up left on the table.—Dan Weatherer

5:00 AM	
6:00 AM	
7:00 AM	
8:00 AM	
9:00 AM	
10:00 AM	
11:00 AM	
12:00 PM	
1:00 PM	
2:00 PM	
3:00 PM	
4:00 PM	
5:00 PM	
6:00 PM	
7:00 PM	
8:00 PM	
9:00 PM	
10:00 PM	
11:00 PM	

Saturday

1/26/2019

Things to Accomplish

_____

_____

_____

_____

Writing Goals

_____

_____

_____

Grab a book. Find a paragraph in the protagonist's POV. Keeping what's on the page, rewrite it from the antagonist's POV. How different is the dialogue, descriptions, tone, etc? It's a good way to see their world view. How differently they see the same world another character has already seen.
—Sheldon Higdon

5:00 AM	
6:00 AM	
7:00 AM	
8:00 AM	
9:00 AM	
10:00 AM	
1:00 AM	
12:00 PM	
1:00 PM	
2:00 PM	
3:00 PM	
4:00 PM	
5:00 PM	
6:00 PM	
7:00 PM	
8:00 PM	
9:00 PM	
10:00 PM	
11:00 PM	

Sunday

1/27/2019

Things to Accomplish

_____

_____

_____

_____

Writing Goals

_____

_____

_____

"Take one hour a week to just sit quietly and think about your goals, projects, and strategies. It'll change your life."—Joe Mynhardt

5:00 AM	
6:00 AM	
7:00 AM	
8:00 AM	
9:00 AM	
10:00 AM	
11:00 AM	
12:00 PM	
1:00 PM	
2:00 PM	
3:00 PM	
4:00 PM	
5:00 PM	
6:00 PM	
7:00 PM	
8:00 PM	
9:00 PM	
10:00 PM	
11:00 PM	

Weekly Planner

_____ to _____

Goals

_____

_____

_____

_____

Notes

MONDAY _____

TUESDAY _____

WEDNESDAY _____

THURSDAY _____

FRIDAY _____

SATURDAY _____

SUNDAY _____

Monday
1/28/2019

Things to Accomplish

_____

_____

_____

_____

Writing Goals

_____

_____

_____

"Writing effectively about the things that live in the dark—the creatures, the evil deeds, fear itself—requires juxtaposition. Never forget the light—the people, their motivations, hope itself—is what makes the darkness frightening. The best horror stories spend time with both."—Ben Fisher

5:00 AM	
6:00 AM	
7:00 AM	
8:00 AM	
9:00 AM	
10:00 AM	
11:00 AM	
12:00 PM	
1:00 PM	
2:00 PM	
3:00 PM	
4:00 PM	
5:00 PM	
6:00 PM	
7:00 PM	
8:00 PM	
9:00 PM	
10:00 PM	
11:00 PM	

Tuesday

1/29/2019

Things to Accomplish

_____

_____

_____

_____

Writing Goals

_____

_____

_____

"Just write every day of your
life. Read intensely. Then see
what happens. Most of my
friends who are put on that
diet have very pleasant
careers."—Ray Bradbury, WD

5:00 AM	
6:00 AM	
7:00 AM	
8:00 AM	
9:00 AM	
10:00 AM	
11:00 AM	
12:00 PM	
1:00 PM	
2:00 PM	
3:00 PM	
4:00 PM	
5:00 PM	
6:00 PM	
7:00 PM	
8:00 PM	
9:00 PM	
10:00 PM	
11:00 PM	

Wednesday

1/30/2019

Things to Accomplish

_____

_____

_____

_____

Writing Goals

_____

_____

_____

After your first draft of a shorter story, print out a copy, sit down, and read the story aloud. Cross out every word you don't need until you're down to the bare bones of the story. This will help you identify necessary words you use too much.—Kenneth W. Cain

5:00 AM
6:00 AM
7:00 AM
8:00 AM
9:00 AM
10:00 AM
11:00 AM
12:00 PM
1:00 PM
2:00 PM
3:00 PM
4:00 PM
5:00 PM
6:00 PM
7:00 PM
8:00 PM
9:00 PM
10:00 PM
11:00 PM

Thursday
1/31/2019

Things to Accomplish

_____

_____

_____

_____

Writing Goals

_____

_____

_____

"If you don't have time to read, you don't have the time (or the tools) to write. Simple as that."—Stephen King

5:00 AM	
6:00 AM	
7:00 AM	
8:00 AM	
9:00 AM	
10:00 AM	
11:00 AM	
12:00 PM	
1:00 PM	
2:00 PM	
3:00 PM	
4:00 PM	
5:00 PM	
6:00 PM	
7:00 PM	
8:00 PM	
9:00 PM	
10:00 PM	
11:00 PM	

Friday

2/1/2019

Things to Accomplish

_____

_____

_____

_____

Writing Goals

_____

_____

_____

"You just have to trust your own madness."—Clive Barker.

5:00 AM	
6:00 AM	
7:00 AM	
8:00 AM	
9:00 AM	
10:00 AM	
11:00 AM	
12:00 PM	
1:00 PM	
2:00 PM	
3:00 PM	
4:00 PM	
5:00 PM	
6:00 PM	
7:00 PM	
8:00 PM	
9:00 PM	
10:00 PM	
11:00 PM	

Saturday

2/2/2019

Things to Accomplish

_____

_____

_____

_____

Writing Goals

_____

_____

_____

"You don't need to compete with anyone. Just write the best story you can and believe in it."—Brian Keene

5:00 AM	
6:00 AM	
7:00 AM	
8:00 AM	
9:00 AM	
10:00 AM	
11:00 AM	
12:00 PM	
1:00 PM	
2:00 PM	
3:00 PM	
4:00 PM	
5:00 PM	
6:00 PM	
7:00 PM	
8:00 PM	
9:00 PM	
10:00 PM	
11:00 PM	

Sunday

2/3/2019

Things to Accomplish

_____

_____

_____

_____

Writing Goals

_____

_____

_____

"Desire and perseverance go a
lot further than raw talent
alone"—Lori Michelle

5:00 AM	
6:00 AM	
7:00 AM	
8:00 AM	
9:00 AM	
10:00 AM	
11:00 AM	
12:00 PM	
1:00 PM	
2:00 PM	
3:00 PM	
4:00 PM	
5:00 PM	
6:00 PM	
7:00 PM	
8:00 PM	
9:00 PM	
10:00 PM	
11:00 PM	

Weekly Planner

_____ to _____

Goals

_____

_____

_____

_____

_____

Notes

MONDAY _____

TUESDAY _____

WEDNESDAY _____

THURSDAY _____

FRIDAY _____

SATURDAY _____

SUNDAY _____

Monday

2/4/2019

Things to Accomplish

_____

_____

_____

_____

Writing Goals

_____

_____

_____

"Half of what I write is garbage, but if I don't write it down it decomposes in my head."—Jarod Kintz,

5:00 AM	
6:00 AM	
7:00 AM	
8:00 AM	
9:00 AM	
10:00 AM	
11:00 AM	
12:00 PM	
1:00 PM	
2:00 PM	
3:00 PM	
4:00 PM	
5:00 PM	
6:00 PM	
7:00 PM	
8:00 PM	
9:00 PM	
10:00 PM	
11:00 PM	

Tuesday

2/5/2019

Things to Accomplish

_____

_____

_____

_____

Writing Goals

_____

_____

_____

"A novelist is a person who lives in other people's skins."— E.L. Doctorow

5:00 AM	
6:00 AM	
7:00 AM	
8:00 AM	
9:00 AM	
10:00 AM	
11:00 AM	
12:00 PM	
1:00 PM	
2:00 PM	
3:00 PM	
4:00 PM	
5:00 PM	
6:00 PM	
7:00 PM	
8:00 PM	
9:00 PM	
10:00 PM	
11:00 PM	

Wednesday

2/6/2019

Things to Accomplish

_____

_____

_____

_____

Writing Goals

_____

_____

_____

Write a poem every day for a month. It can be super short. A few lines, even. It doesn't have to rhyme. It can be freeverse. But tell a story with each poem.—John Palisano

5:00 AM	
6:00 AM	
7:00 AM	
8:00 AM	
9:00 AM	
10:00 AM	
11:00 AM	
12:00 PM	
1:00 PM	
2:00 PM	
3:00 PM	
4:00 PM	
5:00 PM	
6:00 PM	
7:00 PM	
8:00 PM	
9:00 PM	
10:00 PM	
11:00 PM	

Thursday

2/7/2019

Things to Accomplish

_____

_____

_____

_____

Writing Goals

_____

_____

_____

"Good novels are written by
people who are not
frightened."—George Orwell

5:00 AM	
6:00 AM	
7:00 AM	
8:00 AM	
9:00 AM	
10:00 AM	
11:00 AM	
12:00 PM	
1:00 PM	
2:00 PM	
3:00 PM	
4:00 PM	
5:00 PM	
6:00 PM	
7:00 PM	
8:00 PM	
9:00 PM	
10:00 PM	
11:00 PM	

Friday

2/8/2019

Things to Accomplish

_____

_____

_____

_____

Writing Goals

_____

_____

_____

"Two hours of writing fiction leaves this writer completely drained. For those two hours he has been in a different place with totally different people."—Roald Dahl

5:00 AM	
6:00 AM	
7:00 AM	
8:00 AM	
9:00 AM	
10:00 AM	
11:00 AM	
12:00 PM	
1:00 PM	
2:00 PM	
3:00 PM	
4:00 PM	
5:00 PM	
6:00 PM	
7:00 PM	
8:00 PM	
9:00 PM	
10:00 PM	
11:00 PM	

Saturday

2/9/2019

Things to Accomplish

_____

_____

_____

_____

Writing Goals

_____

_____

_____

"Behind every writer stands a very large bookshelf."—Justin Cronin

5:00 AM
6:00 AM
7:00 AM
8:00 AM
9:00 AM
10:00 AM
11:00 AM
12:00 PM
1:00 PM
2:00 PM
3:00 PM
4:00 PM
5:00 PM
6:00 PM
7:00 PM
8:00 PM
9:00 PM
10:00 PM
11:00 PM

Sunday

2/10/2019

Things to Accomplish

_____

_____

_____

_____

Writing Goals

_____

_____

_____

"The best advice I would give new writers is this: write what you love."—Ray Bradbury, in an interview published in Michael McCarty's *Modern Mythmakers*

5:00 AM	
6:00 AM	
7:00 AM	
8:00 AM	
9:00 AM	
10:00 AM	
11:00 AM	
12:00 PM	
1:00 PM	
2:00 PM	
3:00 PM	
4:00 PM	
5:00 PM	
6:00 PM	
7:00 PM	
8:00 PM	
9:00 PM	
10:00 PM	
11:00 PM	

Weekly Planner

_____ to _____

Goals

_____

_____

_____

_____

Notes

MONDAY _____

TUESDAY _____

WEDNESDAY _____

THURSDAY _____

FRIDAY _____

SATURDAY _____

SUNDAY _____

Monday

2/11/2019

Things to Accomplish

_____

_____

_____

_____

Writing Goals

_____

_____

_____

Using only fifty-five words, tell a story. Not a poem, a story. One that has a beginning, a middle and an end. Doing this not only loosens your writing muscles, it also shows you the kind of impact you can achieve with less.—Jonathan Winn

5:00 AM	
6:00 AM	
7:00 AM	
8:00 AM	
9:00 AM	
10:00 AM	
11:00 AM	
12:00 PM	
1:00 PM	
2:00 PM	
3:00 PM	
4:00 PM	
5:00 PM	
6:00 PM	
7:00 PM	
8:00 PM	
9:00 PM	
10:00 PM	
11:00 PM	

Tuesday

2/12/2019

Things to Accomplish

_____

_____

_____

_____

Writing Goals

_____

_____

_____

"If I didn't have writing, I'd be running down the street hurling grenades in people's faces."—Paul Fussell

5:00 AM	
6:00 AM	
7:00 AM	
8:00 AM	
9:00 AM	
10:00 AM	
11:00 AM	
12:00 PM	
1:00 PM	
2:00 PM	
3:00 PM	
4:00 PM	
5:00 PM	
6:00 PM	
7:00 PM	
8:00 PM	
9:00 PM	
10:00 PM	
11:00 PM	

Wednesday

2/13/2019

Things to Accomplish

_____

_____

_____

_____

Writing Goals

_____

_____

_____

"All I need is a sheet of paper
and something to write with,
and then I can turn the world
upside down."
—Friedrich Nietzsche

5:00 AM	
6:00 AM	
7:00 AM	
8:00 AM	
9:00 AM	
10:00 AM	
11:00 AM	
12:00 PM	
1:00 PM	
2:00 PM	
3:00 PM	
4:00 PM	
5:00 PM	
6:00 PM	
7:00 PM	
8:00 PM	
9:00 PM	
10:00 PM	
11:00 PM	

Thursday

2/14/2019

Things to Accomplish

_____

_____

_____

_____

Writing Goals

_____

_____

_____

"If I do not write to empty my mind, I go mad."—George Gordon Byron

5:00 AM	
6:00 AM	
7:00 AM	
8:00 AM	
9:00 AM	
10:00 AM	
1:00 AM	
12:00 PM	
1:00 PM	
2:00 PM	
3:00 PM	
4:00 PM	
5:00 PM	
6:00 PM	
7:00 PM	
8:00 PM	
9:00 PM	
10:00 PM	
11:00 PM	

Friday

2/15/2019

Things to Accomplish

_____

_____

_____

_____

Writing Goals

_____

_____

_____

Wake up every morning and just write a letter longhand. A letter or a short note. It could be to yourself, or your future self, to a loved one or even to death. Do it every day, by hand. No thinking, no editing, just write it, read it and move on with your day.
—Alex Laybourne

5:00 AM	
6:00 AM	
7:00 AM	
8:00 AM	
9:00 AM	
10:00 AM	
11:00 AM	
12:00 PM	
1:00 PM	
2:00 PM	
3:00 PM	
4:00 PM	
5:00 PM	
6:00 PM	
7:00 PM	
8:00 PM	
9:00 PM	
10:00 PM	
11:00 PM	

Saturday

2/16/2019

Things to Accomplish

_____

_____

_____

_____

Writing Goals

_____

_____

_____

"Coming up with ideas is the easiest thing on earth. Putting them down is the hardest."
—Rod Serling

| 5:00 AM |
| 6:00 AM |
| 7:00 AM |
| 8:00 AM |
| 9:00 AM |
| 10:00 AM |
| 11:00 AM |
| 12:00 PM |
| 1:00 PM |
| 2:00 PM |
| 3:00 PM |
| 4:00 PM |
| 5:00 PM |
| 6:00 PM |
| 7:00 PM |
| 8:00 PM |
| 9:00 PM |
| 10:00 PM |
| 11:00 PM |

Sunday

2/17/2019

Things to Accomplish

_____

_____

_____

_____

Writing Goals

_____

_____

_____

"A book is a dream that you
hold in your hands."
—Neil Gaiman

5:00 AM	
6:00 AM	
7:00 AM	
8:00 AM	
9:00 AM	
10:00 AM	
11:00 AM	
12:00 PM	
1:00 PM	
2:00 PM	
3:00 PM	
4:00 PM	
5:00 PM	
6:00 PM	
7:00 PM	
8:00 PM	
9:00 PM	
10:00 PM	
11:00 PM	

Weekly Planner

_____ to _____

Goals

_____

_____

_____

_____

Notes

MONDAY _____

TUESDAY _____

WEDNESDAY _____

THURSDAY _____

FRIDAY _____

SATURDAY _____

SUNDAY _____

Monday

2/18/2019

Things to Accomplish

_____

_____

_____

_____

Writing Goals

_____

_____

_____

"Any word you have to hunt
for in a thesaurus is the wrong
word. There are no exceptions
to this rule."—Stephen King

5:00 AM	
6:00 AM	
7:00 AM	
8:00 AM	
9:00 AM	
10:00 AM	
11:00 AM	
12:00 PM	
1:00 PM	
2:00 PM	
3:00 PM	
4:00 PM	
5:00 PM	
6:00 PM	
7:00 PM	
8:00 PM	
9:00 PM	
10:00 PM	
11:00 PM	

Tuesday

2/19/2019

Things to Accomplish

_____

_____

_____

_____

Writing Goals

_____

_____

_____

"First forget inspiration. Habit is more dependable. Habit will sustain you whether you're inspired or not. Habit will help you finish and polish your stories. Inspiration won't. Habit is persistence in practice."—Octavia E. Butler

5:00 AM	
6:00 AM	
7:00 AM	
8:00 AM	
9:00 AM	
10:00 AM	
11:00 AM	
12:00 PM	
1:00 PM	
2:00 PM	
3:00 PM	
4:00 PM	
5:00 PM	
6:00 PM	
7:00 PM	
8:00 PM	
9:00 PM	
10:00 PM	
11:00 PM	

Wednesday

2/20/2019

Things to Accomplish

_____

_____

_____

_____

Writing Goals

_____

_____

_____

"Somewhere along the way we all go a bit mad. So burn, let go and dive into the horror, because maybe it's the chaos which helps us find where we belong."—Robert M. Drake

5:00 AM	
6:00 AM	
7:00 AM	
8:00 AM	
9:00 AM	
10:00 AM	
11:00 AM	
12:00 PM	
1:00 PM	
2:00 PM	
3:00 PM	
4:00 PM	
5:00 PM	
6:00 PM	
7:00 PM	
8:00 PM	
9:00 PM	
10:00 PM	
11:00 PM	

Thursday

2/21/2019

Things to Accomplish

_____

_____

_____

_____

Writing Goals

_____

_____

_____

"Enjoy your work. The frustration you'll experience sometimes, the feeling that you don't know how to write, may be the birth pangs of something genuinely new. I still suffer that experience. It's preferable to playing safe with a formula. Surprise us, astonish us. Good luck! I look forward to reading you!"—Ramsey Campbell

5:00 AM	
6:00 AM	
7:00 AM	
8:00 AM	
9:00 AM	
10:00 AM	
11:00 AM	
12:00 PM	
1:00 PM	
2:00 PM	
3:00 PM	
4:00 PM	
5:00 PM	
6:00 PM	
7:00 PM	
8:00 PM	
9:00 PM	
10:00 PM	
11:00 PM	

Friday

2/22/2019

Things to Accomplish

_____

_____

_____

_____

Writing Goals

_____

_____

_____

"Be yourself. Avoid self-censorship. Love your failures."—Clive Barker

5:00 AM	
6:00 AM	
7:00 AM	
8:00 AM	
9:00 AM	
10:00 AM	
11:00 AM	
12:00 PM	
1:00 PM	
2:00 PM	
3:00 PM	
4:00 PM	
5:00 PM	
6:00 PM	
7:00 PM	
8:00 PM	
9:00 PM	
10:00 PM	
11:00 PM	

Saturday

2/23/2019

Things to Accomplish

_____

_____

_____

_____

Writing Goals

_____

_____

_____

"Be brave. Go where the pain is. Go where the pleasure is. Seek to create in words the world in which you long to live."—Anne Rice

5:00 AM	
6:00 AM	
7:00 AM	
8:00 AM	
9:00 AM	
10:00 AM	
11:00 AM	
12:00 PM	
1:00 PM	
2:00 PM	
3:00 PM	
4:00 PM	
5:00 PM	
6:00 PM	
7:00 PM	
8:00 PM	
9:00 PM	
10:00 PM	
11:00 PM	

Sunday

2/24/2019

Things to Accomplish

_____

_____

_____

_____

Writing Goals

_____

_____

_____

"The future belongs to those who believe in the beauty of their dreams."
—Eleanor Roosevelt

5:00 AM	
6:00 AM	
7:00 AM	
8:00 AM	
9:00 AM	
10:00 AM	
11:00 AM	
12:00 PM	
1:00 PM	
2:00 PM	
3:00 PM	
4:00 PM	
5:00 PM	
6:00 PM	
7:00 PM	
8:00 PM	
9:00 PM	
10:00 PM	
11:00 PM	

Weekly Planner

_____ to _____

Goals

_____

_____

_____

_____

_____

Notes

MONDAY _____

TUESDAY _____

WEDNESDAY _____

THURSDAY _____

FRIDAY _____

SATURDAY _____

SUNDAY _____

Monday
2/25/2019

Things to Accomplish

_____

_____

_____

_____

Writing Goals

_____

_____

_____

"There is nothing to writing.
All you do is sit down at a
typewriter and bleed."
—Ernest Hemingway

5:00 AM	
6:00 AM	
7:00 AM	
8:00 AM	
9:00 AM	
10:00 AM	
11:00 AM	
12:00 PM	
1:00 PM	
2:00 PM	
3:00 PM	
4:00 PM	
5:00 PM	
6:00 PM	
7:00 PM	
8:00 PM	
9:00 PM	
10:00 PM	
11:00 PM	

Tuesday

2/26/2019

Things to Accomplish

_____

_____

_____

_____

Writing Goals

_____

_____

_____

"I believe man will not merely
endure, he will prevail . . .
because he has a spirit capable
of compassion and sacrifice
and endurance."
—William Faulkner

5:00 AM	
6:00 AM	
7:00 AM	
8:00 AM	
9:00 AM	
10:00 AM	
11:00 AM	
12:00 PM	
1:00 PM	
2:00 PM	
3:00 PM	
4:00 PM	
5:00 PM	
6:00 PM	
7:00 PM	
8:00 PM	
9:00 PM	
10:00 PM	
11:00 PM	

Wednesday

2/27/2019

Things to Accomplish

_____

_____

_____

_____

Writing Goals

_____

_____

_____

"Luck is what happens when preparation meets opportunity."—Seneca

5:00 AM	
6:00 AM	
7:00 AM	
8:00 AM	
9:00 AM	
10:00 AM	
11:00 AM	
12:00 PM	
1:00 PM	
2:00 PM	
3:00 PM	
4:00 PM	
5:00 PM	
6:00 PM	
7:00 PM	
8:00 PM	
9:00 PM	
10:00 PM	
11:00 PM	

Thursday
2/28/2019

Things to Accomplish

_____

_____

_____

_____

Writing Goals

_____

_____

_____

"Opportunity is missed by most people because it is dressed in overalls and looks like work."—Thomas Edison

5:00 AM	
6:00 AM	
7:00 AM	
8:00 AM	
9:00 AM	
10:00 AM	
11:00 AM	
12:00 PM	
1:00 PM	
2:00 PM	
3:00 PM	
4:00 PM	
5:00 PM	
6:00 PM	
7:00 PM	
8:00 PM	
9:00 PM	
10:00 PM	
11:00 PM	

Friday

3/1/2019

Things to Accomplish

_____

_____

_____

_____

Writing Goals

_____

_____

_____

"A professional writer is an amateur who didn't quit."
—Richard Bach

5:00 AM	
6:00 AM	
7:00 AM	
8:00 AM	
9:00 AM	
10:00 AM	
11:00 AM	
12:00 PM	
1:00 PM	
2:00 PM	
3:00 PM	
4:00 PM	
5:00 PM	
6:00 PM	
7:00 PM	
8:00 PM	
9:00 PM	
10:00 PM	
11:00 PM	

Saturday

3/2/2019

Things to Accomplish

_____

_____

_____

_____

Writing Goals

_____

_____

_____

"My motivational quote can be condensed into 2 words: "Don't stop." And then you simply add whatever is necessary at the end. Don't stop believing in yourself. Don't stop trying. Don't stop writing. Don't stop editing. Don't stop learning your craft. Don't stop paying it forward. Just . . . don't ever stop."—J.G. Faherty

| 5:00 AM |
| 6:00 AM |
| 7:00 AM |
| 8:00 AM |
| 9:00 AM |
| 10:00 AM |
| 11:00 AM |
| 12:00 PM |
| 1:00 PM |
| 2:00 PM |
| 3:00 PM |
| 4:00 PM |
| 5:00 PM |
| 6:00 PM |
| 7:00 PM |
| 8:00 PM |
| 9:00 PM |
| 10:00 PM |
| 11:00 PM |

Sunday

3/3/2019

Things to Accomplish

_____

_____

_____

_____

Writing Goals

_____

_____

_____

"Every interesting thing you've experienced in life, good and bad, turn into fiction. Exaggerate, turn bland truths inside out and upside down for others to enjoy. Nobody needs to know where your ideas come from, what's truth and what's a lie. They just need a reason to turn the page. Give them one."
—Chad Lutzke

5:00 AM	
6:00 AM	
7:00 AM	
8:00 AM	
9:00 AM	
10:00 AM	
11:00 AM	
12:00 PM	
1:00 PM	
2:00 PM	
3:00 PM	
4:00 PM	
5:00 PM	
6:00 PM	
7:00 PM	
8:00 PM	
9:00 PM	
10:00 PM	
11:00 PM	

Weekly Planner

_____ to _____

Goals

_____

_____

_____

_____

_____

Notes

MONDAY _____

TUESDAY _____

WEDNESDAY _____

THURSDAY _____

FRIDAY _____

SATURDAY _____

SUNDAY _____

Monday

3/4/2019

Things to Accomplish

_____

_____

_____

_____

Writing Goals

_____

_____

_____

"Let the world burn through
you. Throw the prism light,
white hot, on paper."
—Ray Bradbury

5:00 AM	
6:00 AM	
7:00 AM	
8:00 AM	
9:00 AM	
10:00 AM	
11:00 AM	
12:00 PM	
1:00 PM	
2:00 PM	
3:00 PM	
4:00 PM	
5:00 PM	
6:00 PM	
7:00 PM	
8:00 PM	
9:00 PM	
10:00 PM	
11:00 PM	

Tuesday

3/5/2019

Things to Accomplish

_____

_____

_____

_____

Writing Goals

_____

_____

_____

"When I say work I only mean writing. Everything else is just odd jobs."—Margaret Laurence

5:00 AM	
6:00 AM	
7:00 AM	
8:00 AM	
9:00 AM	
10:00 AM	
11:00 AM	
12:00 PM	
1:00 PM	
2:00 PM	
3:00 PM	
4:00 PM	
5:00 PM	
6:00 PM	
7:00 PM	
8:00 PM	
9:00 PM	
10:00 PM	
11:00 PM	

Wednesday

3/6/2019

Things to Accomplish

_____

_____

_____

_____

Writing Goals

_____

_____

_____

"The difference between the almost right word and the right word is ... the difference between the lightning bug and the lightning."—Mark Twain

5:00 AM	
6:00 AM	
7:00 AM	
8:00 AM	
9:00 AM	
10:00 AM	
11:00 AM	
12:00 PM	
1:00 PM	
2:00 PM	
3:00 PM	
4:00 PM	
5:00 PM	
6:00 PM	
7:00 PM	
8:00 PM	
9:00 PM	
10:00 PM	
11:00 PM	

Thursday

3/7/2019

Things to Accomplish

_____

_____

_____

_____

Writing Goals

_____

_____

_____

"A dream doesn't become reality through magic; it takes sweat, determination and hard work."—Colin Powell

5:00 AM	
6:00 AM	
7:00 AM	
8:00 AM	
9:00 AM	
10:00 AM	
11:00 AM	
12:00 PM	
1:00 PM	
2:00 PM	
3:00 PM	
4:00 PM	
5:00 PM	
6:00 PM	
7:00 PM	
8:00 PM	
9:00 PM	
10:00 PM	
11:00 PM	

Friday

3/8/2019

Things to Accomplish

_____

_____

_____

_____

Writing Goals

_____

_____

_____

"Get it down. Take chances. It may be bad, but it's the only way you can do anything good."—William Faulkner

5:00 AM	
6:00 AM	
7:00 AM	
8:00 AM	
9:00 AM	
10:00 AM	
11:00 AM	
12:00 PM	
1:00 PM	
2:00 PM	
3:00 PM	
4:00 PM	
5:00 PM	
6:00 PM	
7:00 PM	
8:00 PM	
9:00 PM	
10:00 PM	
11:00 PM	

Saturday

3/9/2019

Things to Accomplish

_____

_____

_____

_____

Writing Goals

_____

_____

_____

"I regard each sentence as a little wheel . . . Now and again I try to put a really big one next to a very small one in such a way that the big one, turning slowly, will make the small one spin so fast that it hums. Very tricky, that."—Roald Dahl

5:00 AM	
6:00 AM	
7:00 AM	
8:00 AM	
9:00 AM	
10:00 AM	
11:00 AM	
12:00 PM	
1:00 PM	
2:00 PM	
3:00 PM	
4:00 PM	
5:00 PM	
6:00 PM	
7:00 PM	
8:00 PM	
9:00 PM	
10:00 PM	
11:00 PM	

Sunday

3/10/2019

Things to Accomplish

_____

_____

_____

_____

Writing Goals

_____

_____

_____

"Consider writing in the middle of the night, on the "graveyard shift" It does make a difference in the amount of distractions you avoid and we are writing horror—We don't want the sun shining and birds singing!"
—Brian J. Lewis

5:00 AM	
6:00 AM	
7:00 AM	
8:00 AM	
9:00 AM	
10:00 AM	
11:00 AM	
12:00 PM	
1:00 PM	
2:00 PM	
3:00 PM	
4:00 PM	
5:00 PM	
6:00 PM	
7:00 PM	
8:00 PM	
9:00 PM	
10:00 PM	
11:00 PM	

Weekly Planner

_____ to _____

Goals

_____

_____

_____

_____

_____

Notes

MONDAY _____

TUESDAY _____

WEDNESDAY _____

THURSDAY _____

FRIDAY _____

SATURDAY _____

SUNDAY _____

Monday
3/11/2019

Things to Accomplish

_____

_____

_____

_____

Writing Goals

_____

_____

_____

Some practical advice I learned early on was to understand passive and active voice. A simple trick to find passive sentences is to word-search the word 'was'. I'm serious. 'He was walking'? Change to 'He walked'. Easy.—Matt Hayward

5:00 AM	
6:00 AM	
7:00 AM	
8:00 AM	
9:00 AM	
10:00 AM	
11:00 AM	
12:00 PM	
1:00 PM	
2:00 PM	
3:00 PM	
4:00 PM	
5:00 PM	
6:00 PM	
7:00 PM	
8:00 PM	
9:00 PM	
10:00 PM	
11:00 PM	

Tuesday

3/12/2019

Things to Accomplish

_____

_____

_____

_____

Writing Goals

_____

_____

_____

"It takes courage to open strange doors, stumble into dangerous worlds and look into the eyes of that which scares you. If you've chosen to walk into the dark, it's not because you're weak, but because you're strong."—Jonathan Winn

5:00 AM	
6:00 AM	
7:00 AM	
8:00 AM	
9:00 AM	
10:00 AM	
11:00 AM	
12:00 PM	
1:00 PM	
2:00 PM	
3:00 PM	
4:00 PM	
5:00 PM	
6:00 PM	
7:00 PM	
8:00 PM	
9:00 PM	
10:00 PM	
11:00 PM	

Wednesday

3/13/2019

Things to Accomplish

_____

_____

_____

_____

Writing Goals

_____

_____

_____

"All writing takes guts, and genre writing takes more than most. You have to delve into strange, dark places within yourself to make them real on the page. This act of emotional seppuku isn't something everyone can do, but each story is one only you can tell."—Patrick Rutigliano

5:00 AM	
6:00 AM	
7:00 AM	
8:00 AM	
9:00 AM	
10:00 AM	
11:00 AM	
12:00 PM	
1:00 PM	
2:00 PM	
3:00 PM	
4:00 PM	
5:00 PM	
6:00 PM	
7:00 PM	
8:00 PM	
9:00 PM	
10:00 PM	
11:00 PM	

Thursday

3/14/2019

Things to Accomplish

_____

_____

_____

_____

Writing Goals

_____

_____

_____

"Don't forget—no one else sees
the world the way you do, so
no one else can tell the stories
that you have to tell."
—Charles de Lint

5:00 AM	
6:00 AM	
7:00 AM	
8:00 AM	
9:00 AM	
10:00 AM	
11:00 AM	
12:00 PM	
1:00 PM	
2:00 PM	
3:00 PM	
4:00 PM	
5:00 PM	
6:00 PM	
7:00 PM	
8:00 PM	
9:00 PM	
10:00 PM	
11:00 PM	

Friday

3/15/2019

Things to Accomplish

_____

_____

_____

_____

Writing Goals

_____

_____

_____

"I don't write to get rich, win awards or acquire great reviews. I write to fill the empty spaces in my dark soul."—Michael McCarty

5:00 AM	
6:00 AM	
7:00 AM	
8:00 AM	
9:00 AM	
10:00 AM	
11:00 AM	
12:00 PM	
1:00 PM	
2:00 PM	
3:00 PM	
4:00 PM	
5:00 PM	
6:00 PM	
7:00 PM	
8:00 PM	
9:00 PM	
10:00 PM	
11:00 PM	

Saturday

3/16/2019

Things to Accomplish

_____

_____

_____

_____

Writing Goals

_____

_____

_____

"In the past I was asked what I'd like to be if I could be anything in the world. I said: I'd like to be a writer. How many people actually get to be exactly what they wanted? Not too many. But I did. I'm a writer (and that has nothing to do with selling work, publishing, and winning awards)!"—Gene O'Neill

5:00 AM	
6:00 AM	
7:00 AM	
8:00 AM	
9:00 AM	
10:00 AM	
11:00 AM	
12:00 PM	
1:00 PM	
2:00 PM	
3:00 PM	
4:00 PM	
5:00 PM	
6:00 PM	
7:00 PM	
8:00 PM	
9:00 PM	
10:00 PM	
11:00 PM	

Sunday

3/17/2019

Things to Accomplish

_____

_____

_____

_____

Writing Goals

_____

_____

_____

"If the criticism isn't
constructive, it isn't worth
worrying about."
—Michelle Garza and Melissa
Lason

5:00 AM	
6:00 AM	
7:00 AM	
8:00 AM	
9:00 AM	
10:00 AM	
11:00 AM	
12:00 PM	
1:00 PM	
2:00 PM	
3:00 PM	
4:00 PM	
5:00 PM	
6:00 PM	
7:00 PM	
8:00 PM	
9:00 PM	
10:00 PM	
11:00 PM	

Weekly Planner

_____ to _____

Goals

_____

_____

_____

_____

_____

Notes

MONDAY _____

TUESDAY _____

WEDNESDAY _____

THURSDAY _____

FRIDAY _____

SATURDAY _____

SUNDAY _____

Monday

3/18/2019

Things to Accomplish

_____

_____

_____

Writing Goals

_____

_____

_____

"The difference between a good story and a great story is the editor. Any writer, no matter what their genre, ignores this at their peril."
—Dave Jeffery

5:00 AM	
6:00 AM	
7:00 AM	
8:00 AM	
9:00 AM	
10:00 AM	
11:00 AM	
12:00 PM	
1:00 PM	
2:00 PM	
3:00 PM	
4:00 PM	
5:00 PM	
6:00 PM	
7:00 PM	
8:00 PM	
9:00 PM	
10:00 PM	
11:00 PM	

Tuesday

3/19/2019

Things to Accomplish

_____

_____

_____

_____

Writing Goals

_____

_____

_____

"Write every day. Even if some days it feels like all you are doing us shoveling shit from a sitting position."—Steven King

5:00 AM	
6:00 AM	
7:00 AM	
8:00 AM	
9:00 AM	
10:00 AM	
11:00 AM	
12:00 PM	
1:00 PM	
2:00 PM	
3:00 PM	
4:00 PM	
5:00 PM	
6:00 PM	
7:00 PM	
8:00 PM	
9:00 PM	
10:00 PM	
11:00 PM	

Wednesday

3/20/2019

Things to Accomplish

_____

_____

_____

_____

Writing Goals

_____

_____

_____

"No such thing as spare time, no such thing as free time, no such thing as down time. All you got is life time. Go."
—Henry Rollins

5:00 AM	
6:00 AM	
7:00 AM	
8:00 AM	
9:00 AM	
10:00 AM	
11:00 AM	
12:00 PM	
1:00 PM	
2:00 PM	
3:00 PM	
4:00 PM	
5:00 PM	
6:00 PM	
7:00 PM	
8:00 PM	
9:00 PM	
10:00 PM	
11:00 PM	

Thursday
3/21/2019

Things to Accomplish

_____

_____

_____

_____

Writing Goals

_____

_____

_____

"Some days I am more wolf than woman, and I am still learning how to stop apologizing for my wild."
—Nikita Gill

5:00 AM	
6:00 AM	
7:00 AM	
8:00 AM	
9:00 AM	
10:00 AM	
11:00 AM	
12:00 PM	
1:00 PM	
2:00 PM	
3:00 PM	
4:00 PM	
5:00 PM	
6:00 PM	
7:00 PM	
8:00 PM	
9:00 PM	
10:00 PM	
11:00 PM	

Friday

3/22/2019

Things to Accomplish

_____

_____

_____

_____

Writing Goals

_____

_____

_____

"You can always edit a bad page. You can't edit a blank page."—Jodi Picoult

5:00 AM	
6:00 AM	
7:00 AM	
8:00 AM	
9:00 AM	
10:00 AM	
11:00 AM	
12:00 PM	
1:00 PM	
2:00 PM	
3:00 PM	
4:00 PM	
5:00 PM	
6:00 PM	
7:00 PM	
8:00 PM	
9:00 PM	
10:00 PM	
11:00 PM	

Saturday

3/23/2019

Things to Accomplish

_____

_____

_____

_____

Writing Goals

_____

_____

_____

"Forget all the rules. Forget about being published. Write for yourself and celebrate writing."—Melinda Haynes

5:00 AM	
6:00 AM	
7:00 AM	
8:00 AM	
9:00 AM	
10:00 AM	
11:00 AM	
12:00 PM	
1:00 PM	
2:00 PM	
3:00 PM	
4:00 PM	
5:00 PM	
6:00 PM	
7:00 PM	
8:00 PM	
9:00 PM	
10:00 PM	
11:00 PM	

Sunday

3/24/2019

Things to Accomplish

_____

_____

_____

_____

Writing Goals

_____

_____

_____

"Creative work is often driven by pain."—Cormac McCarthy

5:00 AM	
6:00 AM	
7:00 AM	
8:00 AM	
9:00 AM	
10:00 AM	
11:00 AM	
12:00 PM	
1:00 PM	
2:00 PM	
3:00 PM	
4:00 PM	
5:00 PM	
6:00 PM	
7:00 PM	
8:00 PM	
9:00 PM	
10:00 PM	
11:00 PM	

Weekly Planner

_____ to _____

Goals

_____

_____

_____

_____

_____

Notes

MONDAY _____

TUESDAY _____

WEDNESDAY _____

THURSDAY _____

FRIDAY _____

SATURDAY _____

SUNDAY _____

Monday

3/25/2019

Things to Accomplish

_____

_____

_____

_____

Writing Goals

_____

_____

_____

"A short story must have a single mood and every sentence must build towards it."—Edgar Allen Poe

5:00 AM	
6:00 AM	
7:00 AM	
8:00 AM	
9:00 AM	
10:00 AM	
11:00 AM	
12:00 PM	
1:00 PM	
2:00 PM	
3:00 PM	
4:00 PM	
5:00 PM	
6:00 PM	
7:00 PM	
8:00 PM	
9:00 PM	
10:00 PM	
11:00 PM	

Tuesday
3/26/2019

Things to Accomplish

_____

_____

_____

_____

Writing Goals

_____

_____

_____

"Write or die."—Todd Keisling

5:00 AM
6:00 AM
7:00 AM
8:00 AM
9:00 AM
10:00 AM
1:00 AM
12:00 PM
1:00 PM
2:00 PM
3:00 PM
4:00 PM
5:00 PM
6:00 PM
7:00 PM
8:00 PM
9:00 PM
10:00 PM
11:00 PM

Wednesday

3/27/2019

Things to Accomplish

_____

_____

_____

_____

Writing Goals

_____

_____

_____

"Start writing, no matter
what. The water does not flow
until the faucet is turned on."
—Louis L'Amour

5:00 AM	
6:00 AM	
7:00 AM	
8:00 AM	
9:00 AM	
10:00 AM	
11:00 AM	
12:00 PM	
1:00 PM	
2:00 PM	
3:00 PM	
4:00 PM	
5:00 PM	
6:00 PM	
7:00 PM	
8:00 PM	
9:00 PM	
10:00 PM	
11:00 PM	

Thursday

3/28/2019

Things to Accomplish

_____

_____

_____

_____

Writing Goals

_____

_____

_____

"The writer must have a good imagination to begin with, but the imagination has to be muscular, which means it must be exercised in a disciplined way, day in and day out, by writing, failing, succeeding and revising."—Stephen King

5:00 AM	
6:00 AM	
7:00 AM	
8:00 AM	
9:00 AM	
10:00 AM	
11:00 AM	
12:00 PM	
1:00 PM	
2:00 PM	
3:00 PM	
4:00 PM	
5:00 PM	
6:00 PM	
7:00 PM	
8:00 PM	
9:00 PM	
10:00 PM	
11:00 PM	

Friday

3/29/2019

Things to Accomplish

_____

_____

_____

_____

Writing Goals

_____

_____

_____

"Write your short story as if it were the last chapter of a novel."—Roger Zelazny

5:00 AM	
6:00 AM	
7:00 AM	
8:00 AM	
9:00 AM	
10:00 AM	
11:00 AM	
12:00 PM	
1:00 PM	
2:00 PM	
3:00 PM	
4:00 PM	
5:00 PM	
6:00 PM	
7:00 PM	
8:00 PM	
9:00 PM	
10:00 PM	
11:00 PM	

Saturday

3/30/2019

Things to Accomplish

_____

_____

_____

_____

Writing Goals

_____

_____

_____

"Your intuition knows what to write, so get out of the way."
—Ray Bradbury

5:00 AM	
6:00 AM	
7:00 AM	
8:00 AM	
9:00 AM	
10:00 AM	
11:00 AM	
12:00 PM	
1:00 PM	
2:00 PM	
3:00 PM	
4:00 PM	
5:00 PM	
6:00 PM	
7:00 PM	
8:00 PM	
9:00 PM	
10:00 PM	
11:00 PM	

Sunday

3/31/2019

Things to Accomplish

_____

_____

_____

_____

Writing Goals

_____

_____

_____

"You know that part of your
writing that you question—
That's weird and doesn't fit
neatly into a genre or a mold?
Write more of that. Please."
—Richard Thomas

5:00 AM	
6:00 AM	
7:00 AM	
8:00 AM	
9:00 AM	
10:00 AM	
11:00 AM	
12:00 PM	
1:00 PM	
2:00 PM	
3:00 PM	
4:00 PM	
5:00 PM	
6:00 PM	
7:00 PM	
8:00 PM	
9:00 PM	
10:00 PM	
11:00 PM	

Weekly Planner

_____ to _____

Goals

_____

_____

_____

_____

_____

Notes

MONDAY _____

TUESDAY _____

WEDNESDAY _____

THURSDAY _____

FRIDAY _____

SATURDAY _____

SUNDAY _____

Monday

4/1/2019

Things to Accomplish

_____

_____

_____

_____

Writing Goals

_____

_____

_____

"Perseverance is the hard work you do after you get tired of doing the hard work you already did."—Newt Gingrich

5:00 AM	
6:00 AM	
7:00 AM	
8:00 AM	
9:00 AM	
10:00 AM	
11:00 AM	
12:00 PM	
1:00 PM	
2:00 PM	
3:00 PM	
4:00 PM	
5:00 PM	
6:00 PM	
7:00 PM	
8:00 PM	
9:00 PM	
10:00 PM	
11:00 PM	

Tuesday

4/2/2019

Things to Accomplish

_____

_____

_____

_____

Writing Goals

_____

_____

_____

"Success isn't always about greatness. It's about consistency. Consistent hard work leads to success. Greatness will come."
—Dwayne Johnson

5:00 AM	
6:00 AM	
7:00 AM	
8:00 AM	
9:00 AM	
10:00 AM	
1:00 AM	
12:00 PM	
1:00 PM	
2:00 PM	
3:00 PM	
4:00 PM	
5:00 PM	
6:00 PM	
7:00 PM	
8:00 PM	
9:00 PM	
10:00 PM	
11:00 PM	

Wednesday

4/3/2019

Things to Accomplish

_____

_____

_____

_____

Writing Goals

_____

_____

_____

"Change your life today. Don't gamble on the future, act now, without delay."
—Simone de Beauvoir

5:00 AM	
6:00 AM	
7:00 AM	
8:00 AM	
9:00 AM	
10:00 AM	
11:00 AM	
12:00 PM	
1:00 PM	
2:00 PM	
3:00 PM	
4:00 PM	
5:00 PM	
6:00 PM	
7:00 PM	
8:00 PM	
9:00 PM	
10:00 PM	
11:00 PM	

Thursday

4/4/2019

Things to Accomplish

_____

_____

_____

_____

Writing Goals

_____

_____

_____

"Failure will never overtake
me if my determination to
succeed is strong enough."
—Og Mandino

5:00 AM	
6:00 AM	
7:00 AM	
8:00 AM	
9:00 AM	
10:00 AM	
11:00 AM	
12:00 PM	
1:00 PM	
2:00 PM	
3:00 PM	
4:00 PM	
5:00 PM	
6:00 PM	
7:00 PM	
8:00 PM	
9:00 PM	
10:00 PM	
11:00 PM	

Friday

4/5/2019

Things to Accomplish

_____

_____

_____

_____

Writing Goals

_____

_____

_____

"It does not matter how slowly you go as long as you do not stop."—Confucius

5:00 AM	
6:00 AM	
7:00 AM	
8:00 AM	
9:00 AM	
10:00 AM	
11:00 AM	
12:00 PM	
1:00 PM	
2:00 PM	
3:00 PM	
4:00 PM	
5:00 PM	
6:00 PM	
7:00 PM	
8:00 PM	
9:00 PM	
10:00 PM	
11:00 PM	

Saturday

4/6/2019

Things to Accomplish

_____

_____

_____

_____

Writing Goals

_____

_____

_____

"It always seems impossible
until it's done."
—Nelson Mandela

5:00 AM	
6:00 AM	
7:00 AM	
8:00 AM	
9:00 AM	
10:00 AM	
11:00 AM	
12:00 PM	
1:00 PM	
2:00 PM	
3:00 PM	
4:00 PM	
5:00 PM	
6:00 PM	
7:00 PM	
8:00 PM	
9:00 PM	
10:00 PM	
11:00 PM	

Sunday

4/7/2019

Things to Accomplish

_____

_____

_____

_____

Writing Goals

_____

_____

_____

"Your talent is God's gift to
you. What you do with it is
your gift back to God."
—Leo Buscaglia

5:00 AM	
6:00 AM	
7:00 AM	
8:00 AM	
9:00 AM	
10:00 AM	
11:00 AM	
12:00 PM	
1:00 PM	
2:00 PM	
3:00 PM	
4:00 PM	
5:00 PM	
6:00 PM	
7:00 PM	
8:00 PM	
9:00 PM	
10:00 PM	
11:00 PM	

Now available from Crystal Lake Publishing

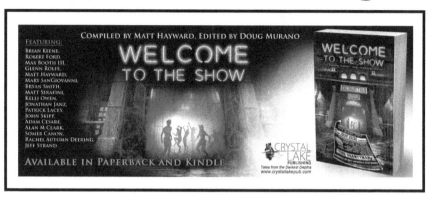

Tales From the Darkest Depths

Weekly Planner

_____ to _____

Goals

_____

_____

_____

_____

_____

Notes

MONDAY _____

TUESDAY _____

WEDNESDAY _____

THURSDAY _____

FRIDAY _____

SATURDAY _____

SUNDAY _____

Monday

4/8/2019

Things to Accomplish

_____

_____

_____

_____

Writing Goals

_____

_____

_____

"You can't cross the sea merely by standing and staring at the water."— Rabindranath Tagore

5:00 AM	
6:00 AM	
7:00 AM	
8:00 AM	
9:00 AM	
10:00 AM	
11:00 AM	
12:00 PM	
1:00 PM	
2:00 PM	
3:00 PM	
4:00 PM	
5:00 PM	
6:00 PM	
7:00 PM	
8:00 PM	
9:00 PM	
10:00 PM	
11:00 PM	

Tuesday

4/9/2019

Things to Accomplish

_____

_____

_____

_____

Writing Goals

_____

_____

_____

"A creative man is motivated by the desire to achieve, not by the desire to beat others."
—Ayn Rand

5:00 AM	
6:00 AM	
7:00 AM	
8:00 AM	
9:00 AM	
10:00 AM	
11:00 AM	
12:00 PM	
1:00 PM	
2:00 PM	
3:00 PM	
4:00 PM	
5:00 PM	
6:00 PM	
7:00 PM	
8:00 PM	
9:00 PM	
10:00 PM	
11:00 PM	

Wednesday
4/10/2019

Things to Accomplish

_____

_____

_____

_____

Writing Goals

_____

_____

_____

"When you can do a common thing in an uncommon way; you will command the attention of the world."
—George Washington Carver

5:00 AM	
6:00 AM	
7:00 AM	
8:00 AM	
9:00 AM	
10:00 AM	
11:00 AM	
12:00 PM	
1:00 PM	
2:00 PM	
3:00 PM	
4:00 PM	
5:00 PM	
6:00 PM	
7:00 PM	
8:00 PM	
9:00 PM	
10:00 PM	
11:00 PM	

Thursday
4/11/2019

Things to Accomplish

_____

_____

_____

_____

Writing Goals

_____

_____

_____

"You can't use up creativity. The more you use, the more you have."—Maya Angelou

5:00 AM	
6:00 AM	
7:00 AM	
8:00 AM	
9:00 AM	
10:00 AM	
11:00 AM	
12:00 PM	
1:00 PM	
2:00 PM	
3:00 PM	
4:00 PM	
5:00 PM	
6:00 PM	
7:00 PM	
8:00 PM	
9:00 PM	
10:00 PM	
11:00 PM	

Friday

4/12/2019

Things to Accomplish

_____

_____

_____

_____

Writing Goals

_____

_____

_____

"The important thing for you is to be alert, to question, to find out, so that your own initiative may be awakened."
—Bruce Lee

5:00 AM	
6:00 AM	
7:00 AM	
8:00 AM	
9:00 AM	
10:00 AM	
11:00 AM	
12:00 PM	
1:00 PM	
2:00 PM	
3:00 PM	
4:00 PM	
5:00 PM	
6:00 PM	
7:00 PM	
8:00 PM	
9:00 PM	
10:00 PM	
11:00 PM	

Saturday

4/13/2019

Things to Accomplish

_____

_____

_____

_____

Writing Goals

_____

_____

_____

"The principal mark of genius
is not perfection but
originality, the opening of new
frontiers."—Arthur Koestler

5:00 AM	
6:00 AM	
7:00 AM	
8:00 AM	
9:00 AM	
10:00 AM	
11:00 AM	
12:00 PM	
1:00 PM	
2:00 PM	
3:00 PM	
4:00 PM	
5:00 PM	
6:00 PM	
7:00 PM	
8:00 PM	
9:00 PM	
10:00 PM	
11:00 PM	

Sunday

4/14/2019

Things to Accomplish

_____

_____

_____

_____

Writing Goals

_____

_____

_____

"Once we believe in ourselves,
we can risk curiosity, wonder,
spontaneous delight or any
experience that reveals the
human spirit."
—E. E. Cummings

5:00 AM	
6:00 AM	
7:00 AM	
8:00 AM	
9:00 AM	
10:00 AM	
1:00 AM	
12:00 PM	
1:00 PM	
2:00 PM	
3:00 PM	
4:00 PM	
5:00 PM	
6:00 PM	
7:00 PM	
8:00 PM	
9:00 PM	
10:00 PM	
11:00 PM	

Weekly Planner

_____ to _____

Goals

_____

_____

_____

_____

Notes

MONDAY _____

TUESDAY _____

WEDNESDAY _____

THURSDAY _____

FRIDAY _____

SATURDAY _____

SUNDAY _____

Monday

4/15/2019

Things to Accomplish

_____

_____

_____

_____

Writing Goals

_____

_____

_____

"The world always seems brighter when you've just made something that wasn't there before."—Neil Gaiman

5:00 AM	
6:00 AM	
7:00 AM	
8:00 AM	
9:00 AM	
10:00 AM	
11:00 AM	
12:00 PM	
1:00 PM	
2:00 PM	
3:00 PM	
4:00 PM	
5:00 PM	
6:00 PM	
7:00 PM	
8:00 PM	
9:00 PM	
10:00 PM	
11:00 PM	

Tuesday
4/16/2019

Things to Accomplish

_____

_____

_____

_____

Writing Goals

_____

_____

_____

"The main thing is to be
moved, to love, to hope, to
tremble, to live."
—Auguste Rodin

5:00 AM	
6:00 AM	
7:00 AM	
8:00 AM	
9:00 AM	
10:00 AM	
1:00 AM	
12:00 PM	
1:00 PM	
2:00 PM	
3:00 PM	
4:00 PM	
5:00 PM	
6:00 PM	
7:00 PM	
8:00 PM	
9:00 PM	
10:00 PM	
11:00 PM	

Wednesday

4/17/2019

Things to Accomplish

_____

_____

_____

_____

Writing Goals

_____

_____

_____

"For me, insanity is super sanity. The normal is psychotic. Normal means lack of imagination, lack of creativity."—Jean Dubuffet

5:00 AM	
6:00 AM	
7:00 AM	
8:00 AM	
9:00 AM	
10:00 AM	
11:00 AM	
12:00 PM	
1:00 PM	
2:00 PM	
3:00 PM	
4:00 PM	
5:00 PM	
6:00 PM	
7:00 PM	
8:00 PM	
9:00 PM	
10:00 PM	
11:00 PM	

Thursday
4/18/2019
Things to Accomplish

_____

_____

_____

_____

Writing Goals

_____

_____

_____

"When I am completely myself, entirely alone during the night when I cannot sleep, it is on such occasions that my ideas flow best and most abundantly."—Mozart

5:00 AM	
6:00 AM	
7:00 AM	
8:00 AM	
9:00 AM	
10:00 AM	
11:00 AM	
12:00 PM	
1:00 PM	
2:00 PM	
3:00 PM	
4:00 PM	
5:00 PM	
6:00 PM	
7:00 PM	
8:00 PM	
9:00 PM	
10:00 PM	
11:00 PM	

Friday

4/19/2019

Things to Accomplish

_____

_____

_____

_____

Writing Goals

_____

_____

_____

Go for a walk or a ride in your neighbourhood. Look about you and choose something innocuous and make a story from it. For example, if you see a discarded sneaker or a felled tree, write a narrative as to how these objects came to be where they are.
—Dave Jeffery

5:00 AM	
6:00 AM	
7:00 AM	
8:00 AM	
9:00 AM	
10:00 AM	
11:00 AM	
12:00 PM	
1:00 PM	
2:00 PM	
3:00 PM	
4:00 PM	
5:00 PM	
6:00 PM	
7:00 PM	
8:00 PM	
9:00 PM	
10:00 PM	
11:00 PM	

Saturday

4/20/2019

Things to Accomplish

_____

_____

_____

_____

Writing Goals

_____

_____

_____

"Work fast enough that you have to trust your gut, but slow enough so that you're proud of the end product."
—Lynne Hansen

5:00 AM	
6:00 AM	
7:00 AM	
8:00 AM	
9:00 AM	
10:00 AM	
11:00 AM	
12:00 PM	
1:00 PM	
2:00 PM	
3:00 PM	
4:00 PM	
5:00 PM	
6:00 PM	
7:00 PM	
8:00 PM	
9:00 PM	
10:00 PM	
11:00 PM	

Sunday
4/21/2019

Things to Accomplish

_____

_____

_____

_____

Writing Goals

_____

_____

_____

"The shadows will come, no matter the pains you take to keep them at bay. Write to illuminate the shadow wolf that stalks you. Those things have teeth, but they back down quickly when you show a little mettle, and what's writing if not a display of courage and fortitude?"
—Christa Carmen

5:00 AM	
6:00 AM	
7:00 AM	
8:00 AM	
9:00 AM	
10:00 AM	
11:00 AM	
12:00 PM	
1:00 PM	
2:00 PM	
3:00 PM	
4:00 PM	
5:00 PM	
6:00 PM	
7:00 PM	
8:00 PM	
9:00 PM	
10:00 PM	
11:00 PM	

Weekly Planner

_____ to _____

Goals

_____

_____

_____

_____

_____

Notes

MONDAY _____

TUESDAY _____

WEDNESDAY _____

THURSDAY _____

FRIDAY _____

SATURDAY _____

SUNDAY _____

Monday

4/22/2019

Things to Accomplish

_____

_____

_____

Writing Goals

_____

_____

_____

"Finish what you're writing.
Whatever you have to do to
finish it, finish it."
—Neil Gaiman

5:00 AM	
6:00 AM	
7:00 AM	
8:00 AM	
9:00 AM	
10:00 AM	
11:00 AM	
12:00 PM	
1:00 PM	
2:00 PM	
3:00 PM	
4:00 PM	
5:00 PM	
6:00 PM	
7:00 PM	
8:00 PM	
9:00 PM	
10:00 PM	
11:00 PM	

Tuesday

4/23/2019

Things to Accomplish

_____

_____

_____

_____

Writing Goals

_____

_____

_____

"Let the inspiration to start the next story motivate you to finish your current work in progress. Beware the habit of jumping from one incomplete story to the next incomplete story."—Joe Mynhardt

5:00 AM	
6:00 AM	
7:00 AM	
8:00 AM	
9:00 AM	
10:00 AM	
11:00 AM	
12:00 PM	
1:00 PM	
2:00 PM	
3:00 PM	
4:00 PM	
5:00 PM	
6:00 PM	
7:00 PM	
8:00 PM	
9:00 PM	
10:00 PM	
11:00 PM	

Wednesday

4/24/2019

Things to Accomplish

_____

_____

_____

_____

Writing Goals

_____

_____

_____

"My darling, you're going to bleed anyway. Take that pain and paint the page with it."
—Mercedes M. Yardley

5:00 AM	
6:00 AM	
7:00 AM	
8:00 AM	
9:00 AM	
10:00 AM	
11:00 AM	
12:00 PM	
1:00 PM	
2:00 PM	
3:00 PM	
4:00 PM	
5:00 PM	
6:00 PM	
7:00 PM	
8:00 PM	
9:00 PM	
10:00 PM	
11:00 PM	

Thursday

4/25/2019

Things to Accomplish

_____

_____

_____

_____

Writing Goals

_____

_____

_____

"Every sentence must do one of two things—reveal character or advance the action."—Kurt Vonnegut

5:00 AM	
6:00 AM	
7:00 AM	
8:00 AM	
9:00 AM	
10:00 AM	
11:00 AM	
12:00 PM	
1:00 PM	
2:00 PM	
3:00 PM	
4:00 PM	
5:00 PM	
6:00 PM	
7:00 PM	
8:00 PM	
9:00 PM	
10:00 PM	
11:00 PM	

Friday

4/26/2019

Things to Accomplish

_____

_____

_____

_____

Writing Goals

_____

_____

_____

Keep an 'ideas' notebook with you
at all times. Specify sections for
novel ideas, short story ideas,
poetry, essays, blogs, and character
names, but also establish a section
for 'images, half-formed ideas,
oddities, etc.' Meld unrelated
images or abstractions together,
and craft a short story from the
most intriguing amalgamation.—

5:00 AM
6:00 AM
7:00 AM
8:00 AM
9:00 AM
10:00 AM
11:00 AM
12:00 PM
1:00 PM
2:00 PM
3:00 PM
4:00 PM
5:00 PM
6:00 PM
7:00 PM
8:00 PM
9:00 PM
10:00 PM
11:00 PM

Saturday

4/27/2019

Things to Accomplish

_____

_____

_____

_____

Writing Goals

_____

_____

_____

Christa Carmen

5:00 AM	
6:00 AM	
7:00 AM	
8:00 AM	
9:00 AM	
10:00 AM	
11:00 AM	
12:00 PM	
1:00 PM	
2:00 PM	
3:00 PM	
4:00 PM	
5:00 PM	
6:00 PM	
7:00 PM	
8:00 PM	
9:00 PM	
10:00 PM	
11:00 PM	

Sunday

4/28/2019

Things to Accomplish

_____

_____

_____

_____

Writing Goals

_____

_____

_____

"Shortcomings and mistakes are only human. Don't allow these to discourage you, but learn from them. Think of yourself as a work-in-progress, and don't fear to strive for the knowledge and skill to be the author you want to be. This is the path to improvement."
—Tommy B. Smith

5:00 AM	
6:00 AM	
7:00 AM	
8:00 AM	
9:00 AM	
10:00 AM	
11:00 AM	
12:00 PM	
1:00 PM	
2:00 PM	
3:00 PM	
4:00 PM	
5:00 PM	
6:00 PM	
7:00 PM	
8:00 PM	
9:00 PM	
10:00 PM	
11:00 PM	

Weekly Planner

_____ to _____

Goals

_____

_____

_____

_____

_____

Notes

MONDAY _____

TUESDAY _____

WEDNESDAY _____

THURSDAY _____

FRIDAY _____

SATURDAY _____

SUNDAY _____

Monday
4/29/2019

Things to Accomplish

_____

_____

_____

_____

Writing Goals

_____

_____

_____

"I'd say it's the same for any kind of writing really, the three P's: Patience, Persistence and Perspiration. Being a good writer in any genre takes time, lots of staying power and lots and lots of hard work!"
—Paul Kane

5:00 AM	
6:00 AM	
7:00 AM	
8:00 AM	
9:00 AM	
10:00 AM	
11:00 AM	
12:00 PM	
1:00 PM	
2:00 PM	
3:00 PM	
4:00 PM	
5:00 PM	
6:00 PM	
7:00 PM	
8:00 PM	
9:00 PM	
10:00 PM	
11:00 PM	

Tuesday

4/30/2019

Things to Accomplish

_____

_____

_____

_____

Writing Goals

_____

_____

_____

"Write whatever speaks to you without judging it (too dark, too raw, etc.) because no one is going to read it but you. Then in rewrite you can decide if you want to share it with the world. This is where you can find the essence of your voice.:"—Linda Addison

5:00 AM	
6:00 AM	
7:00 AM	
8:00 AM	
9:00 AM	
10:00 AM	
11:00 AM	
12:00 PM	
1:00 PM	
2:00 PM	
3:00 PM	
4:00 PM	
5:00 PM	
6:00 PM	
7:00 PM	
8:00 PM	
9:00 PM	
10:00 PM	
11:00 PM	

Wednesday

5/1/2019

Things to Accomplish

_____

_____

_____

_____

Writing Goals

_____

_____

_____

"Writing often feels like taking dictation for the right side of the brain while the left side interrupts with edits. The key is getting a few words in before the battle gets physical." —Rena Mason

5:00 AM	
6:00 AM	
7:00 AM	
8:00 AM	
9:00 AM	
10:00 AM	
11:00 AM	
12:00 PM	
1:00 PM	
2:00 PM	
3:00 PM	
4:00 PM	
5:00 PM	
6:00 PM	
7:00 PM	
8:00 PM	
9:00 PM	
10:00 PM	
11:00 PM	

Thursday

5/2/2019

Things to Accomplish

_____

_____

_____

_____

Writing Goals

_____

_____

_____

Push yourself out of your comfort zone. Take a story you've already written that didn't sell, or that you're not happy with, and rewrite it from a different point of view. A different character, 2nd person instead of 3rd or 1st, or present tense instead of past.
—J.G. Faherty

5:00 AM	
6:00 AM	
7:00 AM	
8:00 AM	
9:00 AM	
10:00 AM	
11:00 AM	
12:00 PM	
1:00 PM	
2:00 PM	
3:00 PM	
4:00 PM	
5:00 PM	
6:00 PM	
7:00 PM	
8:00 PM	
9:00 PM	
10:00 PM	
11:00 PM	

Friday

5/3/2019

Things to Accomplish

_____

_____

_____

_____

Writing Goals

_____

_____

_____

Giving a literary background to random images can help give birth to myriad ideas. I'm not talking about the obvious--pictures of creepy girls with unsettling blank eyes and a dangling Teddy bear in their hand. I mean the unobvious. It's up to you to fill in the blanks.
—Chad Lutzke

5:00 AM	
6:00 AM	
7:00 AM	
8:00 AM	
9:00 AM	
10:00 AM	
11:00 AM	
12:00 PM	
1:00 PM	
2:00 PM	
3:00 PM	
4:00 PM	
5:00 PM	
6:00 PM	
7:00 PM	
8:00 PM	
9:00 PM	
10:00 PM	
11:00 PM	

Saturday

5/4/2019

Things to Accomplish

_____

_____

_____

_____

Writing Goals

_____

_____

_____

"Even if what you're working on doesn't go anywhere, it will help you with the next thin you're doing. Make yourself available for something to happen. Give it a shot."
—Cormac McCarthy

5:00 AM	
6:00 AM	
7:00 AM	
8:00 AM	
9:00 AM	
10:00 AM	
11:00 AM	
12:00 PM	
1:00 PM	
2:00 PM	
3:00 PM	
4:00 PM	
5:00 PM	
6:00 PM	
7:00 PM	
8:00 PM	
9:00 PM	
10:00 PM	
11:00 PM	

Sunday

5/5/2019

Things to Accomplish

_____

_____

_____

_____

Writing Goals

_____

_____

_____

"Do not fear the size of your task but embrace it. The greatest rewards come from the biggest of challenges. Live, love and be challenged daily."—Mark Rippon

5:00 AM	
6:00 AM	
7:00 AM	
8:00 AM	
9:00 AM	
10:00 AM	
11:00 AM	
12:00 PM	
1:00 PM	
2:00 PM	
3:00 PM	
4:00 PM	
5:00 PM	
6:00 PM	
7:00 PM	
8:00 PM	
9:00 PM	
10:00 PM	
11:00 PM	

Weekly Planner

_____ to _____

Goals

_____

_____

_____

_____

_____

Notes

MONDAY _____

TUESDAY _____

WEDNESDAY _____

THURSDAY _____

FRIDAY _____

SATURDAY _____

SUNDAY _____

Monday

5/6/2019

Things to Accomplish

_____

_____

_____

_____

Writing Goals

_____

_____

_____

"There are three important areas to becoming a good writer—talent, luck, and perseverance. With perseverance the most important."—Damon Knight.

5:00 AM	
6:00 AM	
7:00 AM	
8:00 AM	
9:00 AM	
10:00 AM	
11:00 AM	
12:00 PM	
1:00 PM	
2:00 PM	
3:00 PM	
4:00 PM	
5:00 PM	
6:00 PM	
7:00 PM	
8:00 PM	
9:00 PM	
10:00 PM	
11:00 PM	

Tuesday
5/7/2019

Things to Accomplish

_____

_____

_____

_____

Writing Goals

_____

_____

_____

"How far we travel matters less than those we meet along the way."—Mark Twain

5:00 AM	
6:00 AM	
7:00 AM	
8:00 AM	
9:00 AM	
10:00 AM	
11:00 AM	
12:00 PM	
1:00 PM	
2:00 PM	
3:00 PM	
4:00 PM	
5:00 PM	
6:00 PM	
7:00 PM	
8:00 PM	
9:00 PM	
10:00 PM	
11:00 PM	

Wednesday

5/8/2019

Things to Accomplish

_____

_____

_____

_____

Writing Goals

_____

_____

_____

"Life is a challenge to be enjoyed, not a problem to be solved. Be positive, and smile!"—Grant Nicholas

5:00 AM	
6:00 AM	
7:00 AM	
8:00 AM	
9:00 AM	
10:00 AM	
11:00 AM	
12:00 PM	
1:00 PM	
2:00 PM	
3:00 PM	
4:00 PM	
5:00 PM	
6:00 PM	
7:00 PM	
8:00 PM	
9:00 PM	
10:00 PM	
11:00 PM	

Thursday

5/9/2019

Things to Accomplish

_____

_____

_____

_____

Writing Goals

_____

_____

_____

"If we didn't die, life wouldn't
carry such great value and
meaning. And, if we didn't
really live, our deaths become
meaningless as we expire in
obscurity and loneliness."
—Robert Steven Rhine

5:00 AM	
6:00 AM	
7:00 AM	
8:00 AM	
9:00 AM	
10:00 AM	
11:00 AM	
12:00 PM	
1:00 PM	
2:00 PM	
3:00 PM	
4:00 PM	
5:00 PM	
6:00 PM	
7:00 PM	
8:00 PM	
9:00 PM	
10:00 PM	
11:00 PM	

Friday

5/10/2019

Things to Accomplish

_____

_____

_____

_____

Writing Goals

_____

_____

_____

"You learn more from the hard times than you do from the good times."
—Owen Hargreaves

5:00 AM	
6:00 AM	
7:00 AM	
8:00 AM	
9:00 AM	
10:00 AM	
11:00 AM	
12:00 PM	
1:00 PM	
2:00 PM	
3:00 PM	
4:00 PM	
5:00 PM	
6:00 PM	
7:00 PM	
8:00 PM	
9:00 PM	
10:00 PM	
11:00 PM	

Saturday

5/11/2019

Things to Accomplish

_____

_____

_____

_____

Writing Goals

_____

_____

_____

"Intelligence without ambition
is a bird without wings."
—Salvador Dali

5:00 AM	
6:00 AM	
7:00 AM	
8:00 AM	
9:00 AM	
10:00 AM	
1:00 AM	
12:00 PM	
1:00 PM	
2:00 PM	
3:00 PM	
4:00 PM	
5:00 PM	
6:00 PM	
7:00 PM	
8:00 PM	
9:00 PM	
10:00 PM	
11:00 PM	

Sunday

5/12/2019

Things to Accomplish

_____

_____

_____

Writing Goals

_____

_____

_____

"Wherever you go in the world and whatever you do, you have the ability to have your life exactly the way you want it to be, as though it's your own empire."—Tom Delonge

5:00 AM	
6:00 AM	
7:00 AM	
8:00 AM	
9:00 AM	
10:00 AM	
11:00 AM	
12:00 PM	
1:00 PM	
2:00 PM	
3:00 PM	
4:00 PM	
5:00 PM	
6:00 PM	
7:00 PM	
8:00 PM	
9:00 PM	
10:00 PM	
11:00 PM	

Weekly Planner

_____ to _____

Goals

_____

_____

_____

_____

Notes

MONDAY _____

TUESDAY _____

WEDNESDAY _____

THURSDAY _____

FRIDAY _____

SATURDAY _____

SUNDAY _____

Monday
5/13/2019

Things to Accomplish

_____

_____

_____

Writing Goals

_____

_____

_____

"Do not follow where the path may lead, go instead where there is no path and leave a trail."—Ralph Waldo Emerson

5:00 AM	
6:00 AM	
7:00 AM	
8:00 AM	
9:00 AM	
10:00 AM	
11:00 AM	
12:00 PM	
1:00 PM	
2:00 PM	
3:00 PM	
4:00 PM	
5:00 PM	
6:00 PM	
7:00 PM	
8:00 PM	
9:00 PM	
10:00 PM	
11:00 PM	

Tuesday
5/14/2019

Things to Accomplish

_____

_____

_____

_____

Writing Goals

_____

_____

_____

"You don't have to be great to get started, but you have to get started to be great."
—Les Brown

5:00 AM	
6:00 AM	
7:00 AM	
8:00 AM	
9:00 AM	
10:00 AM	
11:00 AM	
12:00 PM	
1:00 PM	
2:00 PM	
3:00 PM	
4:00 PM	
5:00 PM	
6:00 PM	
7:00 PM	
8:00 PM	
9:00 PM	
10:00 PM	
11:00 PM	

Wednesday

5/15/2019

Things to Accomplish

_____

_____

_____

_____

Writing Goals

_____

_____

_____

"The real contest is always between what you've done and what you're capable of doing. You measure yourself against yourself and nobody else."
—Geoffrey Gaberino

5:00 AM	
6:00 AM	
7:00 AM	
8:00 AM	
9:00 AM	
10:00 AM	
11:00 AM	
12:00 PM	
1:00 PM	
2:00 PM	
3:00 PM	
4:00 PM	
5:00 PM	
6:00 PM	
7:00 PM	
8:00 PM	
9:00 PM	
10:00 PM	
11:00 PM	

Thursday
5/16/2019

Things to Accomplish

_____

_____

_____

_____

Writing Goals

_____

_____

_____

"The muse is there. A fantastic storehouse, our complete being. All that is most original lies waiting for us to summon it forth."—Ray Bradbury

5:00 AM	
6:00 AM	
7:00 AM	
8:00 AM	
9:00 AM	
10:00 AM	
11:00 AM	
12:00 PM	
1:00 PM	
2:00 PM	
3:00 PM	
4:00 PM	
5:00 PM	
6:00 PM	
7:00 PM	
8:00 PM	
9:00 PM	
10:00 PM	
11:00 PM	

Friday
5/17/2019

Things to Accomplish

_____

_____

_____

_____

Writing Goals

_____

_____

_____

"Many of life's failures are
people who did not realize
how close they were to success
when they gave up."
—Thomas Edison

5:00 AM	
6:00 AM	
7:00 AM	
8:00 AM	
9:00 AM	
10:00 AM	
11:00 AM	
12:00 PM	
1:00 PM	
2:00 PM	
3:00 PM	
4:00 PM	
5:00 PM	
6:00 PM	
7:00 PM	
8:00 PM	
9:00 PM	
10:00 PM	
11:00 PM	

Saturday

5/18/2019

Things to Accomplish

_____

_____

_____

_____

Writing Goals

_____

_____

_____

"Words are sacred. They deserve respect. If you get the right ones, in the right order, you can nudge the world a little."—Tom Stoppard

5:00 AM	
6:00 AM	
7:00 AM	
8:00 AM	
9:00 AM	
10:00 AM	
11:00 AM	
12:00 PM	
1:00 PM	
2:00 PM	
3:00 PM	
4:00 PM	
5:00 PM	
6:00 PM	
7:00 PM	
8:00 PM	
9:00 PM	
10:00 PM	
11:00 PM	

Sunday

5/19/2019

Things to Accomplish

_____

_____

_____

_____

Writing Goals

_____

_____

_____

"The greatest mistake you can make in life is to continually be afraid you will make one."
—Elbert Hubbard

5:00 AM	
6:00 AM	
7:00 AM	
8:00 AM	
9:00 AM	
10:00 AM	
11:00 AM	
12:00 PM	
1:00 PM	
2:00 PM	
3:00 PM	
4:00 PM	
5:00 PM	
6:00 PM	
7:00 PM	
8:00 PM	
9:00 PM	
10:00 PM	
11:00 PM	

Weekly Planner

_____ to _____

Goals

_____

_____

_____

_____

_____

Notes

MONDAY _____

TUESDAY _____

WEDNESDAY _____

THURSDAY _____

FRIDAY _____

SATURDAY _____

SUNDAY _____

Monday

5/20/2019

Things to Accomplish

_____

_____

_____

_____

Writing Goals

_____

_____

_____

"Conditions are never just right. People who delay action until all factors are favourable are the kind who do nothing."—William Feather

5:00 AM	
6:00 AM	
7:00 AM	
8:00 AM	
9:00 AM	
10:00 AM	
11:00 AM	
12:00 PM	
1:00 PM	
2:00 PM	
3:00 PM	
4:00 PM	
5:00 PM	
6:00 PM	
7:00 PM	
8:00 PM	
9:00 PM	
10:00 PM	
11:00 PM	

Tuesday

5/21/2019

Things to Accomplish

_____

_____

_____

_____

Writing Goals

_____

_____

_____

"Yes, it's hard to write, but it's
harder not to."
—Carl Van Doren

5:00 AM	
6:00 AM	
7:00 AM	
8:00 AM	
9:00 AM	
10:00 AM	
11:00 AM	
12:00 PM	
1:00 PM	
2:00 PM	
3:00 PM	
4:00 PM	
5:00 PM	
6:00 PM	
7:00 PM	
8:00 PM	
9:00 PM	
10:00 PM	
11:00 PM	

Wednesday

5/22/2019

Things to Accomplish

_____

_____

_____

_____

Writing Goals

_____

_____

_____

"When once the itch of
literature comes over a man,
nothing can cure it but the
scratching of a pen."
—Samuel Lover

5:00 AM	
6:00 AM	
7:00 AM	
8:00 AM	
9:00 AM	
10:00 AM	
11:00 AM	
12:00 PM	
1:00 PM	
2:00 PM	
3:00 PM	
4:00 PM	
5:00 PM	
6:00 PM	
7:00 PM	
8:00 PM	
9:00 PM	
10:00 PM	
11:00 PM	

Thursday

5/23/2019

Things to Accomplish

_____

_____

_____

_____

Writing Goals

_____

_____

_____

"It's hell writing and it's hell not writing. The only tolerable state is having just written."
—Robert Hass

5:00 AM	
6:00 AM	
7:00 AM	
8:00 AM	
9:00 AM	
10:00 AM	
11:00 AM	
12:00 PM	
1:00 PM	
2:00 PM	
3:00 PM	
4:00 PM	
5:00 PM	
6:00 PM	
7:00 PM	
8:00 PM	
9:00 PM	
10:00 PM	
11:00 PM	

Friday

5/24/2019

Things to Accomplish

_____

_____

_____

_____

Writing Goals

_____

_____

_____

"If you would not be forgotten,
as soon as you are dead and rotten,
either write things worth reading,
or do things worth the writing."—Benjamin Franklin

5:00 AM	
6:00 AM	
7:00 AM	
8:00 AM	
9:00 AM	
10:00 AM	
11:00 AM	
12:00 PM	
1:00 PM	
2:00 PM	
3:00 PM	
4:00 PM	
5:00 PM	
6:00 PM	
7:00 PM	
8:00 PM	
9:00 PM	
10:00 PM	
11:00 PM	

Saturday

5/25/2019

Things to Accomplish

_____

_____

_____

_____

Writing Goals

_____

_____

_____

"Talent is extremely common.
What is rare is the willingness
to endure the life of the
writer."—Kurt Vonnegut

5:00 AM	
6:00 AM	
7:00 AM	
8:00 AM	
9:00 AM	
10:00 AM	
11:00 AM	
12:00 PM	
1:00 PM	
2:00 PM	
3:00 PM	
4:00 PM	
5:00 PM	
6:00 PM	
7:00 PM	
8:00 PM	
9:00 PM	
10:00 PM	
11:00 PM	

Sunday

5/26/2019

Things to Accomplish

_____

_____

_____

_____

Writing Goals

_____

_____

_____

Too often we sit and wait for story ideas. Look for inspiration, don't wait for it to hit you. Take the first sentence you hear or read in the morning and build a story from it. Let your creativity take ordinary things to whole other realms.—Michelle Garza and Melissa Lason

5:00 AM	
6:00 AM	
7:00 AM	
8:00 AM	
9:00 AM	
10:00 AM	
11:00 AM	
12:00 PM	
1:00 PM	
2:00 PM	
3:00 PM	
4:00 PM	
5:00 PM	
6:00 PM	
7:00 PM	
8:00 PM	
9:00 PM	
10:00 PM	
11:00 PM	

Weekly Planner

_____ to _____

Goals

_____

_____

_____

_____

_____

Notes

MONDAY _____

TUESDAY _____

WEDNESDAY _____

THURSDAY _____

FRIDAY _____

SATURDAY _____

SUNDAY _____

Monday
5/27/2019

Things to Accomplish

_____

_____

_____

_____

Writing Goals

_____

_____

_____

Write a one page description of a character waiting for the rain. Start from a third person far point of view and keep moving closer until you can hear the character's thoughts.—@nmscuri

5:00 AM	
6:00 AM	
7:00 AM	
8:00 AM	
9:00 AM	
10:00 AM	
11:00 AM	
12:00 PM	
1:00 PM	
2:00 PM	
3:00 PM	
4:00 PM	
5:00 PM	
6:00 PM	
7:00 PM	
8:00 PM	
9:00 PM	
10:00 PM	
11:00 PM	

Tuesday

5/28/2019

Things to Accomplish

_____

_____

_____

_____

Writing Goals

_____

_____

_____

Ten Random Words: Pick your favorite book, or a book at random. Close your eyes, open the book to a random page, and point. Repeat ten times. You may omit "a", "the", "and", etc., as well as names.—William Box

5:00 AM	
6:00 AM	
7:00 AM	
8:00 AM	
9:00 AM	
10:00 AM	
11:00 AM	
12:00 PM	
1:00 PM	
2:00 PM	
3:00 PM	
4:00 PM	
5:00 PM	
6:00 PM	
7:00 PM	
8:00 PM	
9:00 PM	
10:00 PM	
11:00 PM	

Wednesday

5/29/2019

Things to Accomplish

_____

_____

_____

_____

Writing Goals

_____

_____

_____

"The easiest thing you can do is this business is quit. It's those that can stick with it in the face of adversity that move on to the next level. Aim high."—Kenneth W. Cain

5:00 AM	
6:00 AM	
7:00 AM	
8:00 AM	
9:00 AM	
10:00 AM	
11:00 AM	
12:00 PM	
1:00 PM	
2:00 PM	
3:00 PM	
4:00 PM	
5:00 PM	
6:00 PM	
7:00 PM	
8:00 PM	
9:00 PM	
10:00 PM	
11:00 PM	

Thursday
5/30/2019

Things to Accomplish

_____

_____

_____

_____

Writing Goals

_____

_____

_____

Lost in Translation: Find a passage in a book. Copy and paste (or type) it into Google Translate. Translate it to another language. Translate that translation (not in English). Repeat eight times. Translate it back to English. Start your story as if the new passage happened just before your beginning.
—William Box

5:00 AM	
6:00 AM	
7:00 AM	
8:00 AM	
9:00 AM	
10:00 AM	
11:00 AM	
12:00 PM	
1:00 PM	
2:00 PM	
3:00 PM	
4:00 PM	
5:00 PM	
6:00 PM	
7:00 PM	
8:00 PM	
9:00 PM	
10:00 PM	
11:00 PM	

Friday

5/31/2019

Things to Accomplish

_____

_____

_____

_____

Writing Goals

_____

_____

_____

"This is the kind of character who . . . " and fill in the blank. "This is the type of character who offers to get you out of those wet clothes when you're perfectly dry."
—Mercedes M. Yardley

5:00 AM	
6:00 AM	
7:00 AM	
8:00 AM	
9:00 AM	
10:00 AM	
11:00 AM	
12:00 PM	
1:00 PM	
2:00 PM	
3:00 PM	
4:00 PM	
5:00 PM	
6:00 PM	
7:00 PM	
8:00 PM	
9:00 PM	
10:00 PM	
11:00 PM	

Saturday

6/1/2019

Things to Accomplish

_____

_____

_____

_____

Writing Goals

_____

_____

_____

Write a few sentences, recasting the chapter you're working on, from the point of view of each of your supporting characters. This will give you some great insights into your work.
—Jasper Bark

5:00 AM	
6:00 AM	
7:00 AM	
8:00 AM	
9:00 AM	
10:00 AM	
11:00 AM	
12:00 PM	
1:00 PM	
2:00 PM	
3:00 PM	
4:00 PM	
5:00 PM	
6:00 PM	
7:00 PM	
8:00 PM	
9:00 PM	
10:00 PM	
11:00 PM	

Sunday

6/2/2019

Things to Accomplish

_____

_____

_____

_____

Writing Goals

_____

_____

_____

"Write. Make Mistakes. Learn.
Repeat (for this is a craft
nobody can master)."
—Alex Laybourne

5:00 AM	
6:00 AM	
7:00 AM	
8:00 AM	
9:00 AM	
10:00 AM	
11:00 AM	
12:00 PM	
1:00 PM	
2:00 PM	
3:00 PM	
4:00 PM	
5:00 PM	
6:00 PM	
7:00 PM	
8:00 PM	
9:00 PM	
10:00 PM	
11:00 PM	

Weekly Planner

_____ to _____

Goals

_____

_____

_____

_____

_____

Notes

MONDAY   _____

TUESDAY   _____

WEDNESDAY   _____

THURSDAY   _____

FRIDAY   _____

SATURDAY   _____

SUNDAY   _____

Monday

6/3/2019

Things to Accomplish

_____

_____

_____

_____

Writing Goals

_____

_____

_____

"Don't have a mindset of just getting things done every day. Don't think about how much progress can make today. It distracts you from turning something that's good into great. It's the only way to deliver more than just average."
—Joe Mynhardt

5:00 AM	
6:00 AM	
7:00 AM	
8:00 AM	
9:00 AM	
10:00 AM	
11:00 AM	
12:00 PM	
1:00 PM	
2:00 PM	
3:00 PM	
4:00 PM	
5:00 PM	
6:00 PM	
7:00 PM	
8:00 PM	
9:00 PM	
10:00 PM	
11:00 PM	

Tuesday
6/4/2019

Things to Accomplish

_____

_____

_____

_____

Writing Goals

_____

_____

_____

"There is no terror in the bang, only in the anticipation of it."—Alfred Hitchcock

5:00 AM	
6:00 AM	
7:00 AM	
8:00 AM	
9:00 AM	
10:00 AM	
1:00 AM	
12:00 PM	
1:00 PM	
2:00 PM	
3:00 PM	
4:00 PM	
5:00 PM	
6:00 PM	
7:00 PM	
8:00 PM	
9:00 PM	
10:00 PM	
11:00 PM	

Wednesday

6/5/2019

Things to Accomplish

_____

_____

_____

_____

Writing Goals

_____

_____

_____

"Lastly, take a drive in the wee hours in the morning for vibe. Even your own city won't feel the same as it does during the day."—Brian J. Lewis

5:00 AM	
6:00 AM	
7:00 AM	
8:00 AM	
9:00 AM	
10:00 AM	
11:00 AM	
12:00 PM	
1:00 PM	
2:00 PM	
3:00 PM	
4:00 PM	
5:00 PM	
6:00 PM	
7:00 PM	
8:00 PM	
9:00 PM	
10:00 PM	
11:00 PM	

Thursday

6/6/2019

Things to Accomplish

_____

_____

_____

_____

Writing Goals

_____

_____

_____

Create a character confronted
by a being or force that
shatters his sanity. Write him
struggling to express what has
happened through physical
action alone.
—Patrick Rutigliano

5:00 AM	
6:00 AM	
7:00 AM	
8:00 AM	
9:00 AM	
10:00 AM	
11:00 AM	
12:00 PM	
1:00 PM	
2:00 PM	
3:00 PM	
4:00 PM	
5:00 PM	
6:00 PM	
7:00 PM	
8:00 PM	
9:00 PM	
10:00 PM	
11:00 PM	

Friday

6/7/2019

Things to Accomplish

_____

_____

_____

_____

Writing Goals

_____

_____

_____

"One day, you will be old enough to start reading fairytales again."—C.S. Lewis

5:00 AM
6:00 AM
7:00 AM
8:00 AM
9:00 AM
10:00 AM
11:00 AM
12:00 PM
1:00 PM
2:00 PM
3:00 PM
4:00 PM
5:00 PM
6:00 PM
7:00 PM
8:00 PM
9:00 PM
10:00 PM
11:00 PM

Saturday

6/8/2019

Things to Accomplish

_____

_____

_____

_____

Writing Goals

_____

_____

_____

"Your stories are yours to tell. It doesn't matter if you're not yet an accomplished writer. In the beginning it doesn't even matter if you haven't yet been able to complete anything. Nobody else can tell your stories."—Steve Rasnic Tem (*Yours to Tell: Dialogues on the Art & Practice of Writing*, Apex Books)

5:00 AM	
6:00 AM	
7:00 AM	
8:00 AM	
9:00 AM	
10:00 AM	
11:00 AM	
12:00 PM	
1:00 PM	
2:00 PM	
3:00 PM	
4:00 PM	
5:00 PM	
6:00 PM	
7:00 PM	
8:00 PM	
9:00 PM	
10:00 PM	
11:00 PM	

Sunday
6/9/2019

Things to Accomplish

_____

_____

_____

_____

Writing Goals

_____

_____

_____

"One day you'll discover that
the opinions of worthless
people are worthless."
—Piers Anthony

5:00 AM	
6:00 AM	
7:00 AM	
8:00 AM	
9:00 AM	
10:00 AM	
11:00 AM	
12:00 PM	
1:00 PM	
2:00 PM	
3:00 PM	
4:00 PM	
5:00 PM	
6:00 PM	
7:00 PM	
8:00 PM	
9:00 PM	
10:00 PM	
11:00 PM	

Weekly Planner

_____ to _____

Goals

_____

_____

_____

_____

_____

Notes

MONDAY _____

TUESDAY _____

WEDNESDAY _____

THURSDAY _____

FRIDAY _____

SATURDAY _____

SUNDAY _____

Monday
6/10/2019

Things to Accomplish

_____

_____

_____

_____

Writing Goals

_____

_____

_____

"I try to create sympathy for
my characters, then turn the
monsters loose."
—Stephen King

5:00 AM	
6:00 AM	
7:00 AM	
8:00 AM	
9:00 AM	
10:00 AM	
11:00 AM	
12:00 PM	
1:00 PM	
2:00 PM	
3:00 PM	
4:00 PM	
5:00 PM	
6:00 PM	
7:00 PM	
8:00 PM	
9:00 PM	
10:00 PM	
11:00 PM	

Tuesday
6/11/2019

Things to Accomplish

_____

_____

_____

_____

Writing Goals

_____

_____

_____

"Any man who keeps working is not a failure. He may not be a great writer, but if he applies the old-fashioned virtues of hard, constant labor, he'll eventually make some kind of career for himself as writer."
—Ray Bradbury

5:00 AM
6:00 AM
7:00 AM
8:00 AM
9:00 AM
10:00 AM
11:00 AM
12:00 PM
1:00 PM
2:00 PM
3:00 PM
4:00 PM
5:00 PM
6:00 PM
7:00 PM
8:00 PM
9:00 PM
10:00 PM
11:00 PM

Wednesday

6/12/2019

Things to Accomplish

_____

_____

_____

_____

Writing Goals

_____

_____

_____

"I have been successful
probably because I have always
realized that I knew nothing
about writing and have merely
tried to tell an interesting story
entertainingly."
—Edgar Rice Burroughs

5:00 AM	
6:00 AM	
7:00 AM	
8:00 AM	
9:00 AM	
10:00 AM	
11:00 AM	
12:00 PM	
1:00 PM	
2:00 PM	
3:00 PM	
4:00 PM	
5:00 PM	
6:00 PM	
7:00 PM	
8:00 PM	
9:00 PM	
10:00 PM	
11:00 PM	

Thursday

6/13/2019

Things to Accomplish

_____

_____

_____

_____

Writing Goals

_____

_____

_____

"First, find out what your hero wants, then just follow him!"—Ray Bradbury

5:00 AM	
6:00 AM	
7:00 AM	
8:00 AM	
9:00 AM	
10:00 AM	
11:00 AM	
12:00 PM	
1:00 PM	
2:00 PM	
3:00 PM	
4:00 PM	
5:00 PM	
6:00 PM	
7:00 PM	
8:00 PM	
9:00 PM	
10:00 PM	
11:00 PM	

Friday
6/14/2019

Things to Accomplish

_____

_____

_____

_____

Writing Goals

_____

_____

_____

"I went for years not finishing anything. Because, of course, when you finish something you can be judged."
—Erica Jong

5:00 AM	
6:00 AM	
7:00 AM	
8:00 AM	
9:00 AM	
10:00 AM	
11:00 AM	
12:00 PM	
1:00 PM	
2:00 PM	
3:00 PM	
4:00 PM	
5:00 PM	
6:00 PM	
7:00 PM	
8:00 PM	
9:00 PM	
10:00 PM	
11:00 PM	

Saturday

6/15/2019

Things to Accomplish

_____

_____

_____

_____

Writing Goals

_____

_____

_____

"Begin with an individual, and
before you know it you have
created a type; begin with a
type, and you find you have
created—nothing."
—F. Scott Fitzgerald

5:00 AM	
6:00 AM	
7:00 AM	
8:00 AM	
9:00 AM	
10:00 AM	
11:00 AM	
12:00 PM	
1:00 PM	
2:00 PM	
3:00 PM	
4:00 PM	
5:00 PM	
6:00 PM	
7:00 PM	
8:00 PM	
9:00 PM	
10:00 PM	
11:00 PM	

Sunday

6/16/2019

Things to Accomplish

_____

_____

_____

_____

Writing Goals

_____

_____

_____

"You learn by writing short
stories. Keep writing short
stories. The money's in novels,
but writing short stories keeps
your writing lean and
pointed."—Larry Niven

5:00 AM	
6:00 AM	
7:00 AM	
8:00 AM	
9:00 AM	
10:00 AM	
11:00 AM	
12:00 PM	
1:00 PM	
2:00 PM	
3:00 PM	
4:00 PM	
5:00 PM	
6:00 PM	
7:00 PM	
8:00 PM	
9:00 PM	
10:00 PM	
11:00 PM	

Weekly Planner

_____ to _____

Goals

_____

_____

_____

_____

_____

Notes

MONDAY _____

TUESDAY _____

WEDNESDAY _____

THURSDAY _____

FRIDAY _____

SATURDAY _____

SUNDAY _____

Monday

6/17/2019

Things to Accomplish

_____

_____

_____

_____

Writing Goals

_____

_____

_____

"Great is the art of beginning,
but greater is the art of
ending."
—Henry Wadsworth
Longfellow

5:00 AM	
6:00 AM	
7:00 AM	
8:00 AM	
9:00 AM	
10:00 AM	
11:00 AM	
12:00 PM	
1:00 PM	
2:00 PM	
3:00 PM	
4:00 PM	
5:00 PM	
6:00 PM	
7:00 PM	
8:00 PM	
9:00 PM	
10:00 PM	
11:00 PM	

Tuesday
6/18/2019

Things to Accomplish

_____

_____

_____

_____

Writing Goals

_____

_____

_____

"If you write one story, it may be bad; if you write a hundred, you have the odds in your favor."—Edgar Rice Burroughs

5:00 AM	
6:00 AM	
7:00 AM	
8:00 AM	
9:00 AM	
10:00 AM	
11:00 AM	
12:00 PM	
1:00 PM	
2:00 PM	
3:00 PM	
4:00 PM	
5:00 PM	
6:00 PM	
7:00 PM	
8:00 PM	
9:00 PM	
10:00 PM	
11:00 PM	

Wednesday

6/19/2019

Things to Accomplish

_____

_____

_____

_____

Writing Goals

_____

_____

_____

"The thing that lies at the foundation of positive change, the way I see it, is service to a fellow human being."
—Lee Iacocca

5:00 AM	
6:00 AM	
7:00 AM	
8:00 AM	
9:00 AM	
10:00 AM	
11:00 AM	
12:00 PM	
1:00 PM	
2:00 PM	
3:00 PM	
4:00 PM	
5:00 PM	
6:00 PM	
7:00 PM	
8:00 PM	
9:00 PM	
10:00 PM	
11:00 PM	

Thursday
6/20/2019

Things to Accomplish

_____

_____

_____

_____

Writing Goals

_____

_____

_____

"Individual science fiction stories may seem as trivial as ever to the blinder critics and philosophers of today—but the core of science fiction, its essence, the concept around which it revolves, has become crucial to our salvation if we are to be saved at all."
—Isaac Asimov

5:00 AM	
6:00 AM	
7:00 AM	
8:00 AM	
9:00 AM	
10:00 AM	
11:00 AM	
12:00 PM	
1:00 PM	
2:00 PM	
3:00 PM	
4:00 PM	
5:00 PM	
6:00 PM	
7:00 PM	
8:00 PM	
9:00 PM	
10:00 PM	
11:00 PM	

Friday

6/21/2019

Things to Accomplish

_____

_____

_____

_____

Writing Goals

_____

_____

_____

"You don't have to burn books to destroy a culture. Just get people to stop reading."
—Ray Bradbury

5:00 AM	
6:00 AM	
7:00 AM	
8:00 AM	
9:00 AM	
10:00 AM	
11:00 AM	
12:00 PM	
1:00 PM	
2:00 PM	
3:00 PM	
4:00 PM	
5:00 PM	
6:00 PM	
7:00 PM	
8:00 PM	
9:00 PM	
10:00 PM	
11:00 PM	

Saturday

6/22/2019

Things to Accomplish

_____

_____

_____

_____

Writing Goals

_____

_____

_____

Think of something you'd like to write about, give yourself five minutes, and come up with 100 words on your chosen idea. Then, if you've got five more minutes, polish those 100 words. Bonus points for more words!—Lisa Morton

5:00 AM	
6:00 AM	
7:00 AM	
8:00 AM	
9:00 AM	
10:00 AM	
11:00 AM	
12:00 PM	
1:00 PM	
2:00 PM	
3:00 PM	
4:00 PM	
5:00 PM	
6:00 PM	
7:00 PM	
8:00 PM	
9:00 PM	
10:00 PM	
11:00 PM	

Sunday

6/23/2019

Things to Accomplish

_____

_____

_____

_____

Writing Goals

_____

_____

_____

"If you think this Universe is bad, you should see some of the others."—Philip K. Dick

5:00 AM	
6:00 AM	
7:00 AM	
8:00 AM	
9:00 AM	
10:00 AM	
11:00 AM	
12:00 PM	
1:00 PM	
2:00 PM	
3:00 PM	
4:00 PM	
5:00 PM	
6:00 PM	
7:00 PM	
8:00 PM	
9:00 PM	
10:00 PM	
11:00 PM	

Weekly Planner

_____ to _____

Goals

_____

_____

_____

_____

_____

Notes

MONDAY _____

TUESDAY _____

WEDNESDAY _____

THURSDAY _____

FRIDAY _____

SATURDAY _____

SUNDAY _____

Monday

6/24/2019

Things to Accomplish

_____

_____

_____

_____

Writing Goals

_____

_____

_____

"Show me a completely
smooth operation and I'll
show you someone who's
covering mistakes. Real boats
rock." —Frank Herbert,
excerpt from *Dune*

5:00 AM	
6:00 AM	
7:00 AM	
8:00 AM	
9:00 AM	
10:00 AM	
11:00 AM	
12:00 PM	
1:00 PM	
2:00 PM	
3:00 PM	
4:00 PM	
5:00 PM	
6:00 PM	
7:00 PM	
8:00 PM	
9:00 PM	
10:00 PM	
11:00 PM	

Tuesday

6/25/2019

Things to Accomplish

_____

_____

_____

_____

Writing Goals

_____

_____

_____

Writing exercise (from Yours to Tell: Dialogues on the Art & Practice of Writing, Apex Books): as practice in POV, retell the same short story from different characters within the story, or from the same character but from first and then third person. As you explore the story from a different point of view, you might make the happy discovery that there's another story to be told as well as the one you thought you were working on.—Steve Rasnic Tem

5:00 AM	
6:00 AM	
7:00 AM	
8:00 AM	
9:00 AM	
10:00 AM	
11:00 AM	
12:00 PM	
1:00 PM	
2:00 PM	
3:00 PM	
4:00 PM	
5:00 PM	
6:00 PM	
7:00 PM	
8:00 PM	
9:00 PM	
10:00 PM	
11:00 PM	

Wednesday

6/26/2019

Things to Accomplish

_____

_____

_____

_____

Writing Goals

_____

_____

_____

"You've a story to tell, so treat your first draft as an outline, not as an intended finished product. Embrace the flaws; they will still be there for the crucial re-write, which is where your story will begin to take its final form."

5:00 AM	
6:00 AM	
7:00 AM	
8:00 AM	
9:00 AM	
10:00 AM	
11:00 AM	
12:00 PM	
1:00 PM	
2:00 PM	
3:00 PM	
4:00 PM	
5:00 PM	
6:00 PM	
7:00 PM	
8:00 PM	
9:00 PM	
10:00 PM	
11:00 PM	

Thursday

6/27/2019

Things to Accomplish

_____

_____

_____

_____

Writing Goals

_____

_____

_____

—Dan Weatherer

5:00 AM	
6:00 AM	
7:00 AM	
8:00 AM	
9:00 AM	
10:00 AM	
1:00 AM	
12:00 PM	
1:00 PM	
2:00 PM	
3:00 PM	
4:00 PM	
5:00 PM	
6:00 PM	
7:00 PM	
8:00 PM	
9:00 PM	
10:00 PM	
11:00 PM	

Friday

6/28/2019

Things to Accomplish

_____

_____

_____

Writing Goals

_____

_____

_____

"The path of least resistance is
the path of the loser."
—H.G. Wells

5:00 AM	
6:00 AM	
7:00 AM	
8:00 AM	
9:00 AM	
10:00 AM	
11:00 AM	
12:00 PM	
1:00 PM	
2:00 PM	
3:00 PM	
4:00 PM	
5:00 PM	
6:00 PM	
7:00 PM	
8:00 PM	
9:00 PM	
10:00 PM	
11:00 PM	

Saturday

6/29/2019

Things to Accomplish

_____

_____

_____

_____

Writing Goals

_____

_____

_____

"Get inside their skin. That includes even the ones who are complete bastards, nasty, twisted, deeply flawed human beings with serious psychological problems. Even them."—George R.R. Martin

| 5:00 AM |
| 6:00 AM |
| 7:00 AM |
| 8:00 AM |
| 9:00 AM |
| 10:00 AM |
| 11:00 AM |
| 12:00 PM |
| 1:00 PM |
| 2:00 PM |
| 3:00 PM |
| 4:00 PM |
| 5:00 PM |
| 6:00 PM |
| 7:00 PM |
| 8:00 PM |
| 9:00 PM |
| 10:00 PM |
| 11:00 PM |

Sunday

6/30/2019

Things to Accomplish

_____

_____

_____

_____

Writing Goals

_____

_____

_____

"Listen to the way people talk.
If your characters sound real
the rest is easy."
—David Eddings

5:00 AM	
6:00 AM	
7:00 AM	
8:00 AM	
9:00 AM	
10:00 AM	
11:00 AM	
12:00 PM	
1:00 PM	
2:00 PM	
3:00 PM	
4:00 PM	
5:00 PM	
6:00 PM	
7:00 PM	
8:00 PM	
9:00 PM	
10:00 PM	
11:00 PM	

Weekly Planner

_____ to _____

Goals

_____

_____

_____

_____

Notes

MONDAY _____

TUESDAY _____

WEDNESDAY _____

THURSDAY _____

FRIDAY _____

SATURDAY _____

SUNDAY _____

Monday

7/1/2019

Things to Accomplish

_____

_____

_____

_____

Writing Goals

_____

_____

_____

Think about the title of your favorite song. Now write a flash fiction story of exactly two hundred words.
—Joe Mynhardt

5:00 AM	
6:00 AM	
7:00 AM	
8:00 AM	
9:00 AM	
10:00 AM	
11:00 AM	
12:00 PM	
1:00 PM	
2:00 PM	
3:00 PM	
4:00 PM	
5:00 PM	
6:00 PM	
7:00 PM	
8:00 PM	
9:00 PM	
10:00 PM	
11:00 PM	

Tuesday

7/2/2019

Things to Accomplish

_____

_____

_____

_____

Writing Goals

_____

_____

_____

"Creativity is piercing the mundane to find the marvelous."—Bill Moyers

5:00 AM	
6:00 AM	
7:00 AM	
8:00 AM	
9:00 AM	
10:00 AM	
11:00 AM	
12:00 PM	
1:00 PM	
2:00 PM	
3:00 PM	
4:00 PM	
5:00 PM	
6:00 PM	
7:00 PM	
8:00 PM	
9:00 PM	
10:00 PM	
11:00 PM	

Wednesday
7/3/2019
Things to Accomplish

_____

_____

_____

_____

Writing Goals

_____

_____

_____

"Creativity is contagious. Pass it on."—Albert Einstein

5:00 AM	
6:00 AM	
7:00 AM	
8:00 AM	
9:00 AM	
10:00 AM	
11:00 AM	
12:00 PM	
1:00 PM	
2:00 PM	
3:00 PM	
4:00 PM	
5:00 PM	
6:00 PM	
7:00 PM	
8:00 PM	
9:00 PM	
10:00 PM	
11:00 PM	

Thursday

7/4/2019

Things to Accomplish

_____

_____

_____

_____

Writing Goals

_____

_____

_____

"Be yourself. Everyone else is already taken."—Oscar Wilde

5:00 AM	
6:00 AM	
7:00 AM	
8:00 AM	
9:00 AM	
10:00 AM	
11:00 AM	
12:00 PM	
1:00 PM	
2:00 PM	
3:00 PM	
4:00 PM	
5:00 PM	
6:00 PM	
7:00 PM	
8:00 PM	
9:00 PM	
10:00 PM	
11:00 PM	

Friday

7/5/2019

Things to Accomplish

_____

_____

_____

_____

Writing Goals

_____

_____

_____

"The great use of life is to spend it for something that will outlast it."
—William James

5:00 AM	
6:00 AM	
7:00 AM	
8:00 AM	
9:00 AM	
10:00 AM	
11:00 AM	
12:00 PM	
1:00 PM	
2:00 PM	
3:00 PM	
4:00 PM	
5:00 PM	
6:00 PM	
7:00 PM	
8:00 PM	
9:00 PM	
10:00 PM	
11:00 PM	

Saturday
7/6/2019

Things to Accomplish

_____

_____

_____

_____

Writing Goals

_____

_____

_____

"Inspiration does exist, but it must find you working."
—Pablo Picasso

5:00 AM	
6:00 AM	
7:00 AM	
8:00 AM	
9:00 AM	
10:00 AM	
11:00 AM	
12:00 PM	
1:00 PM	
2:00 PM	
3:00 PM	
4:00 PM	
5:00 PM	
6:00 PM	
7:00 PM	
8:00 PM	
9:00 PM	
10:00 PM	
11:00 PM	

Sunday

7/7/2019

Things to Accomplish

_____

_____

_____

_____

Writing Goals

_____

_____

_____

I always say if you're having problems with dialogue, interview your characters. Write questions and then, as the character, answer them in writing. It's amazing how it helps you find that character's voice.—Jonathan Winn

5:00 AM	
6:00 AM	
7:00 AM	
8:00 AM	
9:00 AM	
10:00 AM	
11:00 AM	
12:00 PM	
1:00 PM	
2:00 PM	
3:00 PM	
4:00 PM	
5:00 PM	
6:00 PM	
7:00 PM	
8:00 PM	
9:00 PM	
10:00 PM	
11:00 PM	

Weekly Planner

_____ to _____

Goals

_____

_____

_____

_____

_____

Notes

MONDAY _____

TUESDAY _____

WEDNESDAY _____

THURSDAY _____

FRIDAY _____

SATURDAY _____

SUNDAY _____

Monday

7/8/2019

Things to Accomplish

_____

_____

_____

_____

Writing Goals

_____

_____

_____

Choose something utterly
mundane—corn chips,
lipstick—and write a short
horror story featuring that
object or person as the
centerpiece.—Ben Fisher

5:00 AM	
6:00 AM	
7:00 AM	
8:00 AM	
9:00 AM	
10:00 AM	
11:00 AM	
12:00 PM	
1:00 PM	
2:00 PM	
3:00 PM	
4:00 PM	
5:00 PM	
6:00 PM	
7:00 PM	
8:00 PM	
9:00 PM	
10:00 PM	
11:00 PM	

Tuesday

7/9/2019

Things to Accomplish

_____

_____

_____

_____

Writing Goals

_____

_____

_____

"There are chords in the hearts of the most reckless which cannot be touched without emotion."—Edgar Allan Poe

5:00 AM	
6:00 AM	
7:00 AM	
8:00 AM	
9:00 AM	
10:00 AM	
11:00 AM	
12:00 PM	
1:00 PM	
2:00 PM	
3:00 PM	
4:00 PM	
5:00 PM	
6:00 PM	
7:00 PM	
8:00 PM	
9:00 PM	
10:00 PM	
11:00 PM	

Wednesday

7/10/2019

Things to Accomplish

_____

_____

_____

_____

Writing Goals

_____

_____

_____

"There is no greater agony than bearing an untold story inside you."—Maya Angelou

5:00 AM	
6:00 AM	
7:00 AM	
8:00 AM	
9:00 AM	
10:00 AM	
11:00 AM	
12:00 PM	
1:00 PM	
2:00 PM	
3:00 PM	
4:00 PM	
5:00 PM	
6:00 PM	
7:00 PM	
8:00 PM	
9:00 PM	
10:00 PM	
11:00 PM	

Thursday
7/11/2019

Things to Accomplish

_____

_____

_____

_____

Writing Goals

_____

_____

_____

"You must stay drunk on
writing so reality cannot
destroy you"—Ray Bradbury

5:00 AM	
6:00 AM	
7:00 AM	
8:00 AM	
9:00 AM	
10:00 AM	
11:00 AM	
12:00 PM	
1:00 PM	
2:00 PM	
3:00 PM	
4:00 PM	
5:00 PM	
6:00 PM	
7:00 PM	
8:00 PM	
9:00 PM	
10:00 PM	
11:00 PM	

Friday

7/12/2019

Things to Accomplish

_____

_____

_____

_____

Writing Goals

_____

_____

_____

"Nothing is so embarrassing
as watching someone do
something that you said
couldn't be done."
—Sam Ewing

5:00 AM	
6:00 AM	
7:00 AM	
8:00 AM	
9:00 AM	
10:00 AM	
11:00 AM	
12:00 PM	
1:00 PM	
2:00 PM	
3:00 PM	
4:00 PM	
5:00 PM	
6:00 PM	
7:00 PM	
8:00 PM	
9:00 PM	
10:00 PM	
11:00 PM	

Saturday

7/13/2019

Things to Accomplish

_____

_____

_____

_____

Writing Goals

_____

_____

_____

"One day I will find the right words, and they will be simple."—Jack Kerouac, *The Dharma Bums*

5:00 AM	
6:00 AM	
7:00 AM	
8:00 AM	
9:00 AM	
10:00 AM	
11:00 AM	
12:00 PM	
1:00 PM	
2:00 PM	
3:00 PM	
4:00 PM	
5:00 PM	
6:00 PM	
7:00 PM	
8:00 PM	
9:00 PM	
10:00 PM	
11:00 PM	

Sunday

7/14/2019

Things to Accomplish

_____

_____

_____

_____

Writing Goals

_____

_____

_____

"Either write something worth reading or do something worth writing."
—Benjamin Franklin

5:00 AM	
6:00 AM	
7:00 AM	
8:00 AM	
9:00 AM	
10:00 AM	
11:00 AM	
12:00 PM	
1:00 PM	
2:00 PM	
3:00 PM	
4:00 PM	
5:00 PM	
6:00 PM	
7:00 PM	
8:00 PM	
9:00 PM	
10:00 PM	
11:00 PM	

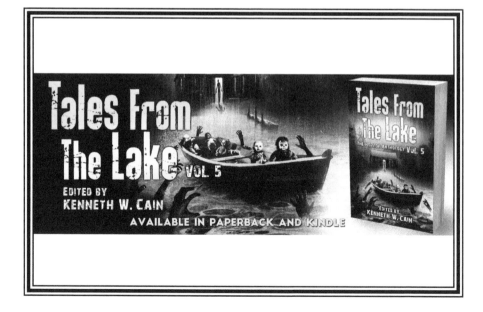

"This beautifully macabre collection of urban legends and ghastly encounters is a cold whisper, a dripping axe, a shattered camera lens. Walk carefully into Carmen's night. But if you hear flies, run."
—Stephanie M. Wytovich
Bram Stoker award-winning author of *Brothel*

"Christa Carmen is undoubtedly one of horror's most exciting and distinctive new voices."
—Gwendolyn Kiste, Author of *And Her Smile Will Untether the Universe*

"A gorgeous foray into the dark inner world."
—Christina Sng
Bram Stoker award-winning author of *A Collection of Nightmares*

Weekly Planner

_____ to _____

Goals

_____

_____

_____

_____

_____

Notes

MONDAY _____

TUESDAY _____

WEDNESDAY _____

THURSDAY _____

FRIDAY _____

SATURDAY _____

SUNDAY _____

Monday
7/15/2019
Things to Accomplish

_____

_____

_____

_____

Writing Goals

_____

_____

_____

"No tears in the writer, no tears in the reader. No surprise in the writer, no surprise in the reader."
—Robert Frost

5:00 AM	
6:00 AM	
7:00 AM	
8:00 AM	
9:00 AM	
10:00 AM	
11:00 AM	
12:00 PM	
1:00 PM	
2:00 PM	
3:00 PM	
4:00 PM	
5:00 PM	
6:00 PM	
7:00 PM	
8:00 PM	
9:00 PM	
10:00 PM	
11:00 PM	

Tuesday

7/16/2019

Things to Accomplish

_____

_____

_____

_____

Writing Goals

_____

_____

_____

"Read, read, read. Read everything—trash, classics, good and bad, and see how they do it. Just like a carpenter who works as an apprentice and studies the master. Read! You'll absorb it. Then write. If it's good, you'll find out. If it's not, throw it out of the window."—William Faulkner

5:00 AM	
6:00 AM	
7:00 AM	
8:00 AM	
9:00 AM	
10:00 AM	
11:00 AM	
12:00 PM	
1:00 PM	
2:00 PM	
3:00 PM	
4:00 PM	
5:00 PM	
6:00 PM	
7:00 PM	
8:00 PM	
9:00 PM	
10:00 PM	
11:00 PM	

Wednesday

7/17/2019

Things to Accomplish

_____

_____

_____

_____

Writing Goals

_____

_____

_____

"You must stay drunk on writing so reality cannot destroy you."—Ray Bradbury, *Zen in the Art of Writing*

5:00 AM	
6:00 AM	
7:00 AM	
8:00 AM	
9:00 AM	
10:00 AM	
11:00 AM	
12:00 PM	
1:00 PM	
2:00 PM	
3:00 PM	
4:00 PM	
5:00 PM	
6:00 PM	
7:00 PM	
8:00 PM	
9:00 PM	
10:00 PM	
11:00 PM	

Thursday
7/18/2019

Things to Accomplish

_____

_____

_____

_____

Writing Goals

_____

_____

_____

"Words can be like X-rays if you use them properly—they'll go through anything. You read and you're pierced."
—Aldous Huxley

5:00 AM	
6:00 AM	
7:00 AM	
8:00 AM	
9:00 AM	
10:00 AM	
11:00 AM	
12:00 PM	
1:00 PM	
2:00 PM	
3:00 PM	
4:00 PM	
5:00 PM	
6:00 PM	
7:00 PM	
8:00 PM	
9:00 PM	
10:00 PM	
11:00 PM	

Friday

7/19/2019

Things to Accomplish

_____

_____

_____

_____

Writing Goals

_____

_____

_____

"How vain it is to sit down to write when you have not stood up to live."
—Henry David Thoreau

5:00 AM	
6:00 AM	
7:00 AM	
8:00 AM	
9:00 AM	
10:00 AM	
1:00 AM	
12:00 PM	
1:00 PM	
2:00 PM	
3:00 PM	
4:00 PM	
5:00 PM	
6:00 PM	
7:00 PM	
8:00 PM	
9:00 PM	
10:00 PM	
11:00 PM	

Saturday
7/20/2019

Things to Accomplish

_____

_____

_____

_____

Writing Goals

_____

_____

_____

"I can shake off everything as I
write; my sorrows disappear,
my courage is reborn."
—Anne Frank

5:00 AM	
6:00 AM	
7:00 AM	
8:00 AM	
9:00 AM	
10:00 AM	
11:00 AM	
12:00 PM	
1:00 PM	
2:00 PM	
3:00 PM	
4:00 PM	
5:00 PM	
6:00 PM	
7:00 PM	
8:00 PM	
9:00 PM	
10:00 PM	
11:00 PM	

Sunday

7/21/2019

Things to Accomplish

_____

_____

_____

_____

Writing Goals

_____

_____

_____

"A writer is someone for whom writing is more difficult than it is for other people."
—Thomas Mann

5:00 AM	
6:00 AM	
7:00 AM	
8:00 AM	
9:00 AM	
10:00 AM	
11:00 AM	
12:00 PM	
1:00 PM	
2:00 PM	
3:00 PM	
4:00 PM	
5:00 PM	
6:00 PM	
7:00 PM	
8:00 PM	
9:00 PM	
10:00 PM	
11:00 PM	

Weekly Planner

_____ to _____

Goals

_____

_____

_____

_____

Notes

MONDAY _____

TUESDAY _____

WEDNESDAY _____

THURSDAY _____

FRIDAY _____

SATURDAY _____

SUNDAY _____

Monday

7/22/2019

Things to Accomplish

_____

_____

_____

_____

Writing Goals

_____

_____

_____

"Don't bend; don't water it
down; don't try to make it
logical; don't edit your own soul
according to the fashion.
Rather, follow your most
intense obsessions
mercilessly."—Franz Kafka

5:00 AM	
6:00 AM	
7:00 AM	
8:00 AM	
9:00 AM	
10:00 AM	
11:00 AM	
12:00 PM	
1:00 PM	
2:00 PM	
3:00 PM	
4:00 PM	
5:00 PM	
6:00 PM	
7:00 PM	
8:00 PM	
9:00 PM	
10:00 PM	
11:00 PM	

Tuesday
7/23/2019

Things to Accomplish

_____

_____

_____

_____

Writing Goals

_____

_____

_____

"I kept always two books in my pocket, one to read, one to write in."
—Robert Louis Stevenson

5:00 AM	
6:00 AM	
7:00 AM	
8:00 AM	
9:00 AM	
10:00 AM	
11:00 AM	
12:00 PM	
1:00 PM	
2:00 PM	
3:00 PM	
4:00 PM	
5:00 PM	
6:00 PM	
7:00 PM	
8:00 PM	
9:00 PM	
10:00 PM	
11:00 PM	

Wednesday

7/24/2019

Things to Accomplish

_____

_____

_____

_____

Writing Goals

_____

_____

_____

"You can make anything by writing."—C.S. Lewis

5:00 AM	
6:00 AM	
7:00 AM	
8:00 AM	
9:00 AM	
10:00 AM	
11:00 AM	
12:00 PM	
1:00 PM	
2:00 PM	
3:00 PM	
4:00 PM	
5:00 PM	
6:00 PM	
7:00 PM	
8:00 PM	
9:00 PM	
10:00 PM	
11:00 PM	

Thursday
7/25/2019

Things to Accomplish

_____

_____

_____

_____

Writing Goals

_____

_____

_____

"A word after a word after a
word is power."
—Margaret Atwood

5:00 AM	
6:00 AM	
7:00 AM	
8:00 AM	
9:00 AM	
10:00 AM	
11:00 AM	
12:00 PM	
1:00 PM	
2:00 PM	
3:00 PM	
4:00 PM	
5:00 PM	
6:00 PM	
7:00 PM	
8:00 PM	
9:00 PM	
10:00 PM	
11:00 PM	

Friday

7/26/2019

Things to Accomplish

_____

_____

_____

_____

Writing Goals

_____

_____

_____

"Tears are words that need to be written."—Paulo Coelho

5:00 AM	
6:00 AM	
7:00 AM	
8:00 AM	
9:00 AM	
10:00 AM	
11:00 AM	
12:00 PM	
1:00 PM	
2:00 PM	
3:00 PM	
4:00 PM	
5:00 PM	
6:00 PM	
7:00 PM	
8:00 PM	
9:00 PM	
10:00 PM	
11:00 PM	

Saturday

7/27/2019

Things to Accomplish

_____

_____

_____

_____

Writing Goals

_____

_____

_____

"I write to discover what I
know."—Flannery O'Connor

5:00 AM	
6:00 AM	
7:00 AM	
8:00 AM	
9:00 AM	
10:00 AM	
11:00 AM	
12:00 PM	
1:00 PM	
2:00 PM	
3:00 PM	
4:00 PM	
5:00 PM	
6:00 PM	
7:00 PM	
8:00 PM	
9:00 PM	
10:00 PM	
11:00 PM	

Sunday

7/28/2019

Things to Accomplish

_____

_____

_____

_____

Writing Goals

_____

_____

_____

"Ideas are like rabbits. You get a couple and learn how to handle them, and pretty soon you have a dozen."
—John Steinbeck

5:00 AM	
6:00 AM	
7:00 AM	
8:00 AM	
9:00 AM	
10:00 AM	
11:00 AM	
12:00 PM	
1:00 PM	
2:00 PM	
3:00 PM	
4:00 PM	
5:00 PM	
6:00 PM	
7:00 PM	
8:00 PM	
9:00 PM	
10:00 PM	
11:00 PM	

Weekly Planner

_____ to _____

Goals

_____

_____

_____

_____

Notes

MONDAY _____

TUESDAY _____

WEDNESDAY _____

THURSDAY _____

FRIDAY _____

SATURDAY _____

SUNDAY _____

Monday
7/29/2019

Things to Accomplish

_____

_____

_____

_____

Writing Goals

_____

_____

_____

"As a writer, you should not judge, you should understand."
—Ernest Hemingway

5:00 AM	
6:00 AM	
7:00 AM	
8:00 AM	
9:00 AM	
10:00 AM	
11:00 AM	
12:00 PM	
1:00 PM	
2:00 PM	
3:00 PM	
4:00 PM	
5:00 PM	
6:00 PM	
7:00 PM	
8:00 PM	
9:00 PM	
10:00 PM	
11:00 PM	

Tuesday
7/30/2019

Things to Accomplish

_____

_____

_____

_____

Writing Goals

_____

_____

_____

"The most valuable of all talents is that of never using two words when one will do."—Thomas Jefferson

5:00 AM	
6:00 AM	
7:00 AM	
8:00 AM	
9:00 AM	
10:00 AM	
11:00 AM	
12:00 PM	
1:00 PM	
2:00 PM	
3:00 PM	
4:00 PM	
5:00 PM	
6:00 PM	
7:00 PM	
8:00 PM	
9:00 PM	
10:00 PM	
11:00 PM	

Wednesday

7/31/2019

Things to Accomplish

_____

_____

_____

_____

Writing Goals

_____

_____

_____

"Get it down. Take chances. It may be bad, but it's the only way you can do anything really good."—William Faulkner

5:00 AM	
6:00 AM	
7:00 AM	
8:00 AM	
9:00 AM	
10:00 AM	
11:00 AM	
12:00 PM	
1:00 PM	
2:00 PM	
3:00 PM	
4:00 PM	
5:00 PM	
6:00 PM	
7:00 PM	
8:00 PM	
9:00 PM	
10:00 PM	
11:00 PM	

Thursday

8/1/2019

Things to Accomplish

_____

_____

_____

_____

Writing Goals

_____

_____

_____

"The road to hell is paved with works-in-progress."
—Philip Roth

5:00 AM	
6:00 AM	
7:00 AM	
8:00 AM	
9:00 AM	
10:00 AM	
11:00 AM	
12:00 PM	
1:00 PM	
2:00 PM	
3:00 PM	
4:00 PM	
5:00 PM	
6:00 PM	
7:00 PM	
8:00 PM	
9:00 PM	
10:00 PM	
11:00 PM	

Friday

8/2/2019

Things to Accomplish

_____

_____

_____

_____

Writing Goals

_____

_____

_____

"Know your literary tradition, savor it, steal from it, but when you sit down to write, forget about worshiping greatness and fetishizing masterpieces."
—Allegra Goodman

5:00 AM	
6:00 AM	
7:00 AM	
8:00 AM	
9:00 AM	
10:00 AM	
11:00 AM	
12:00 PM	
1:00 PM	
2:00 PM	
3:00 PM	
4:00 PM	
5:00 PM	
6:00 PM	
7:00 PM	
8:00 PM	
9:00 PM	
10:00 PM	
11:00 PM	

Saturday

8/3/2019

Things to Accomplish

_____

_____

_____

_____

Writing Goals

_____

_____

_____

"I do not over-intellectualise the production process. I try to keep it simple: Tell the damned story."—Tom Clancy

5:00 AM	
6:00 AM	
7:00 AM	
8:00 AM	
9:00 AM	
10:00 AM	
11:00 AM	
12:00 PM	
1:00 PM	
2:00 PM	
3:00 PM	
4:00 PM	
5:00 PM	
6:00 PM	
7:00 PM	
8:00 PM	
9:00 PM	
10:00 PM	
11:00 PM	

Sunday

8/4/2019

Things to Accomplish

_____

_____

_____

_____

Writing Goals

_____

_____

_____

"I don't need an alarm clock.
My ideas wake me."
—Ray Bradbury

5:00 AM	
6:00 AM	
7:00 AM	
8:00 AM	
9:00 AM	
10:00 AM	
11:00 AM	
12:00 PM	
1:00 PM	
2:00 PM	
3:00 PM	
4:00 PM	
5:00 PM	
6:00 PM	
7:00 PM	
8:00 PM	
9:00 PM	
10:00 PM	
11:00 PM	

Weekly Planner

_____ to _____

Goals

_____

_____

_____

_____

_____

Notes

MONDAY _____

TUESDAY _____

WEDNESDAY _____

THURSDAY _____

FRIDAY _____

SATURDAY _____

SUNDAY _____

Monday

8/5/2019

Things to Accomplish

_____

_____

_____

_____

Writing Goals

_____

_____

_____

Describe yourself from the point of view of your three closest friends.
—Joe Mynhardt

5:00 AM	
6:00 AM	
7:00 AM	
8:00 AM	
9:00 AM	
10:00 AM	
11:00 AM	
12:00 PM	
1:00 PM	
2:00 PM	
3:00 PM	
4:00 PM	
5:00 PM	
6:00 PM	
7:00 PM	
8:00 PM	
9:00 PM	
10:00 PM	
11:00 PM	

Tuesday
8/6/2019

Things to Accomplish

_____

_____

_____

_____

Writing Goals

_____

_____

_____

"Success is not final. Failure is not fatal. It is the courage to continue that counts."
—Winston Churchill

5:00 AM	
6:00 AM	
7:00 AM	
8:00 AM	
9:00 AM	
10:00 AM	
11:00 AM	
12:00 PM	
1:00 PM	
2:00 PM	
3:00 PM	
4:00 PM	
5:00 PM	
6:00 PM	
7:00 PM	
8:00 PM	
9:00 PM	
10:00 PM	
11:00 PM	

Wednesday

8/7/2019

Things to Accomplish

_____

_____

_____

_____

Writing Goals

_____

_____

_____

"There is more treasure in books than in all the pirate's loot on Treasure Island."
—Walt Disney

5:00 AM	
6:00 AM	
7:00 AM	
8:00 AM	
9:00 AM	
10:00 AM	
11:00 AM	
12:00 PM	
1:00 PM	
2:00 PM	
3:00 PM	
4:00 PM	
5:00 PM	
6:00 PM	
7:00 PM	
8:00 PM	
9:00 PM	
10:00 PM	
11:00 PM	

Thursday

8/8/2019

Things to Accomplish

_____

_____

_____

_____

Writing Goals

_____

_____

_____

"Either you're a writer or
you're not, there's no such
thing as an 'aspiring writer.'"
—Monique Snyman

5:00 AM	
6:00 AM	
7:00 AM	
8:00 AM	
9:00 AM	
10:00 AM	
11:00 AM	
12:00 PM	
1:00 PM	
2:00 PM	
3:00 PM	
4:00 PM	
5:00 PM	
6:00 PM	
7:00 PM	
8:00 PM	
9:00 PM	
10:00 PM	
11:00 PM	

Friday

8/9/2019

Things to Accomplish

_____

_____

_____

_____

Writing Goals

_____

_____

_____

Write your last name backwards at the top of a page. You must invent a creature by this name and describe it using all five senses.—Jenn Loring

5:00 AM	
6:00 AM	
7:00 AM	
8:00 AM	
9:00 AM	
10:00 AM	
11:00 AM	
12:00 PM	
1:00 PM	
2:00 PM	
3:00 PM	
4:00 PM	
5:00 PM	
6:00 PM	
7:00 PM	
8:00 PM	
9:00 PM	
10:00 PM	
11:00 PM	

Saturday

8/10/2019

Things to Accomplish

_____

_____

_____

_____

Writing Goals

_____

_____

_____

Do something today that scares you. Face that fear and end the day with a one page reflection. Allow the emotions to flow through your fingers.

5:00 AM	
6:00 AM	
7:00 AM	
8:00 AM	
9:00 AM	
10:00 AM	
11:00 AM	
12:00 PM	
1:00 PM	
2:00 PM	
3:00 PM	
4:00 PM	
5:00 PM	
6:00 PM	
7:00 PM	
8:00 PM	
9:00 PM	
10:00 PM	
11:00 PM	

Sunday

8/11/2019

Things to Accomplish

_____

_____

_____

_____

Writing Goals

_____

_____

_____

"You can't use up creativity.
The more you use, the more
you have."
—Maya Angelou

5:00 AM	
6:00 AM	
7:00 AM	
8:00 AM	
9:00 AM	
10:00 AM	
11:00 AM	
12:00 PM	
1:00 PM	
2:00 PM	
3:00 PM	
4:00 PM	
5:00 PM	
6:00 PM	
7:00 PM	
8:00 PM	
9:00 PM	
10:00 PM	
11:00 PM	

Weekly Planner

_____ to _____

Goals

_____

_____

_____

_____

Notes

MONDAY _____

TUESDAY _____

WEDNESDAY _____

THURSDAY _____

FRIDAY _____

SATURDAY _____

SUNDAY _____

Monday

8/12/2019

Things to Accomplish

_____

_____

_____

_____

Writing Goals

_____

_____

_____

Rewrite the most emotional or
embarrassing conversation
you've ever had.

5:00 AM	
6:00 AM	
7:00 AM	
8:00 AM	
9:00 AM	
10:00 AM	
11:00 AM	
12:00 PM	
1:00 PM	
2:00 PM	
3:00 PM	
4:00 PM	
5:00 PM	
6:00 PM	
7:00 PM	
8:00 PM	
9:00 PM	
10:00 PM	
11:00 PM	

Tuesday

8/13/2019

Things to Accomplish

_____

_____

_____

_____

Writing Goals

_____

_____

_____

Describe your current surrounding from the point of the view of your favorite fictional antagonist.

5:00 AM	
6:00 AM	
7:00 AM	
8:00 AM	
9:00 AM	
10:00 AM	
11:00 AM	
12:00 PM	
1:00 PM	
2:00 PM	
3:00 PM	
4:00 PM	
5:00 PM	
6:00 PM	
7:00 PM	
8:00 PM	
9:00 PM	
10:00 PM	
11:00 PM	

Wednesday

8/14/2019

Things to Accomplish

_____

_____

_____

_____

Writing Goals

_____

_____

_____

"We may sit in our library and yet be in all quarters of the earth."—John Lubbock

5:00 AM	
6:00 AM	
7:00 AM	
8:00 AM	
9:00 AM	
10:00 AM	
11:00 AM	
12:00 PM	
1:00 PM	
2:00 PM	
3:00 PM	
4:00 PM	
5:00 PM	
6:00 PM	
7:00 PM	
8:00 PM	
9:00 PM	
10:00 PM	
11:00 PM	

Thursday

8/15/2019

Things to Accomplish

_____

_____

_____

_____

Writing Goals

_____

_____

_____

Pay it forward today by
helping out at least one other
author/artist out there.

5:00 AM	
6:00 AM	
7:00 AM	
8:00 AM	
9:00 AM	
10:00 AM	
11:00 AM	
12:00 PM	
1:00 PM	
2:00 PM	
3:00 PM	
4:00 PM	
5:00 PM	
6:00 PM	
7:00 PM	
8:00 PM	
9:00 PM	
10:00 PM	
11:00 PM	

Friday

8/16/2019

Things to Accomplish

_____

_____

_____

_____

Writing Goals

_____

_____

_____

"Success is not final, failure is
not fatal: it is the courage to
continue that counts."
—Winston Churchill

5:00 AM	
6:00 AM	
7:00 AM	
8:00 AM	
9:00 AM	
10:00 AM	
11:00 AM	
12:00 PM	
1:00 PM	
2:00 PM	
3:00 PM	
4:00 PM	
5:00 PM	
6:00 PM	
7:00 PM	
8:00 PM	
9:00 PM	
10:00 PM	
11:00 PM	

Saturday

8/17/2019

Things to Accomplish

_____

_____

_____

_____

Writing Goals

_____

_____

_____

"Remember your dreams and fight for them. You must know what you want from life. There is just one thing that makes your dream become impossible: the fear of failure."—Paulo Coelho

5:00 AM	
6:00 AM	
7:00 AM	
8:00 AM	
9:00 AM	
10:00 AM	
11:00 AM	
12:00 PM	
1:00 PM	
2:00 PM	
3:00 PM	
4:00 PM	
5:00 PM	
6:00 PM	
7:00 PM	
8:00 PM	
9:00 PM	
10:00 PM	
11:00 PM	

Sunday

8/18/2019

Things to Accomplish

_____

_____

_____

_____

Writing Goals

_____

_____

_____

"You build on failure. You use it as a stepping stone. Close the door on the past. You don't try to forget the mistakes, but you don't dwell on it. You don't let it have any of your energy, or any of your time, or any of your space."
—Johnny Cash

5:00 AM	
6:00 AM	
7:00 AM	
8:00 AM	
9:00 AM	
10:00 AM	
11:00 AM	
12:00 PM	
1:00 PM	
2:00 PM	
3:00 PM	
4:00 PM	
5:00 PM	
6:00 PM	
7:00 PM	
8:00 PM	
9:00 PM	
10:00 PM	
11:00 PM	

Weekly Planner

_____ to _____

Goals

_____

_____

_____

_____

_____

Notes

MONDAY _____

TUESDAY _____

WEDNESDAY _____

THURSDAY _____

FRIDAY _____

SATURDAY _____

SUNDAY _____

Monday

8/19/2019

Things to Accomplish

_____

_____

_____

_____

Writing Goals

_____

_____

_____

Write a one page character profile of a person battling the fight between good and evil within him/herself.

5:00 AM	
6:00 AM	
7:00 AM	
8:00 AM	
9:00 AM	
10:00 AM	
11:00 AM	
12:00 PM	
1:00 PM	
2:00 PM	
3:00 PM	
4:00 PM	
5:00 PM	
6:00 PM	
7:00 PM	
8:00 PM	
9:00 PM	
10:00 PM	
11:00 PM	

Tuesday

8/20/2019

Things to Accomplish

_____

_____

_____

_____

Writing Goals

_____

_____

_____

"Success consists of going from failure to failure without loss of enthusiasm."
—Winston Churchill

5:00 AM	
6:00 AM	
7:00 AM	
8:00 AM	
9:00 AM	
10:00 AM	
11:00 AM	
12:00 PM	
1:00 PM	
2:00 PM	
3:00 PM	
4:00 PM	
5:00 PM	
6:00 PM	
7:00 PM	
8:00 PM	
9:00 PM	
10:00 PM	
11:00 PM	

Wednesday

8/21/2019

Things to Accomplish

_____

_____

_____

_____

Writing Goals

_____

_____

_____

"Gratitude unlocks the fullness of life. It turns what we have into enough, and more. It turns denial into acceptance, chaos to order, confusion to clarity. It can turn a meal into a feast, a house into a home, a stranger into a friend."
—Melody Beattie

5:00 AM	
6:00 AM	
7:00 AM	
8:00 AM	
9:00 AM	
10:00 AM	
11:00 AM	
12:00 PM	
1:00 PM	
2:00 PM	
3:00 PM	
4:00 PM	
5:00 PM	
6:00 PM	
7:00 PM	
8:00 PM	
9:00 PM	
10:00 PM	
11:00 PM	

Thursday

8/22/2019

Things to Accomplish

_____

_____

_____

_____

Writing Goals

_____

_____

_____

Stream of consciousness—grab an empty paper and just write without thinking.

5:00 AM	
6:00 AM	
7:00 AM	
8:00 AM	
9:00 AM	
10:00 AM	
11:00 AM	
12:00 PM	
1:00 PM	
2:00 PM	
3:00 PM	
4:00 PM	
5:00 PM	
6:00 PM	
7:00 PM	
8:00 PM	
9:00 PM	
10:00 PM	
11:00 PM	

Friday

8/23/2019

Things to Accomplish

_____

_____

_____

_____

Writing Goals

_____

_____

_____

"When something is
important enough, you do it
even if the odds are not in
your favor."
—Elon Musk

5:00 AM	
6:00 AM	
7:00 AM	
8:00 AM	
9:00 AM	
10:00 AM	
1:00 AM	
12:00 PM	
1:00 PM	
2:00 PM	
3:00 PM	
4:00 PM	
5:00 PM	
6:00 PM	
7:00 PM	
8:00 PM	
9:00 PM	
10:00 PM	
11:00 PM	

Saturday

8/24/2019

Things to Accomplish

_____

_____

_____

_____

Writing Goals

_____

_____

_____

"Perseverance is not a long race; it is many short races one after the other."
—Walter Elliot

5:00 AM	
6:00 AM	
7:00 AM	
8:00 AM	
9:00 AM	
10:00 AM	
11:00 AM	
12:00 PM	
1:00 PM	
2:00 PM	
3:00 PM	
4:00 PM	
5:00 PM	
6:00 PM	
7:00 PM	
8:00 PM	
9:00 PM	
10:00 PM	
11:00 PM	

Sunday

8/25/2019

Things to Accomplish

_____

_____

_____

_____

Writing Goals

_____

_____

_____

"Either you run the day or the day runs you."—Jim Rohn

5:00 AM	
6:00 AM	
7:00 AM	
8:00 AM	
9:00 AM	
10:00 AM	
1:00 AM	
12:00 PM	
1:00 PM	
2:00 PM	
3:00 PM	
4:00 PM	
5:00 PM	
6:00 PM	
7:00 PM	
8:00 PM	
9:00 PM	
10:00 PM	
11:00 PM	

Weekly Planner

_____ to _____

Goals

_____

_____

_____

_____

_____

Notes

MONDAY _____

TUESDAY _____

WEDNESDAY _____

THURSDAY _____

FRIDAY _____

SATURDAY _____

SUNDAY _____

Monday

8/26/2019

Things to Accomplish

_____

_____

_____

_____

Writing Goals

_____

_____

_____

"Don't watch the clock; do
what it does. Keep going."
—Sam Levenson

5:00 AM	
6:00 AM	
7:00 AM	
8:00 AM	
9:00 AM	
10:00 AM	
11:00 AM	
12:00 PM	
1:00 PM	
2:00 PM	
3:00 PM	
4:00 PM	
5:00 PM	
6:00 PM	
7:00 PM	
8:00 PM	
9:00 PM	
10:00 PM	
11:00 PM	

Tuesday

8/27/2019

Things to Accomplish

_____

_____

_____

_____

Writing Goals

_____

_____

_____

"What you get by achieving
your goals is not as important
as what you become by
achieving your goals."
—Zig Ziglar

5:00 AM	
6:00 AM	
7:00 AM	
8:00 AM	
9:00 AM	
10:00 AM	
11:00 AM	
12:00 PM	
1:00 PM	
2:00 PM	
3:00 PM	
4:00 PM	
5:00 PM	
6:00 PM	
7:00 PM	
8:00 PM	
9:00 PM	
10:00 PM	
11:00 PM	

Wednesday

8/28/2019

Things to Accomplish

_____

_____

_____

_____

Writing Goals

_____

_____

_____

"Your positive action
combined with positive
thinking results in success."
—Shiv Khera

5:00 AM	
6:00 AM	
7:00 AM	
8:00 AM	
9:00 AM	
10:00 AM	
11:00 AM	
12:00 PM	
1:00 PM	
2:00 PM	
3:00 PM	
4:00 PM	
5:00 PM	
6:00 PM	
7:00 PM	
8:00 PM	
9:00 PM	
10:00 PM	
11:00 PM	

Thursday

8/29/2019

Things to Accomplish

_____

_____

_____

_____

Writing Goals

_____

_____

_____

Write a flash fiction piece about someone sneaking through your window at this very moment.

5:00 AM	
6:00 AM	
7:00 AM	
8:00 AM	
9:00 AM	
10:00 AM	
11:00 AM	
12:00 PM	
1:00 PM	
2:00 PM	
3:00 PM	
4:00 PM	
5:00 PM	
6:00 PM	
7:00 PM	
8:00 PM	
9:00 PM	
10:00 PM	
11:00 PM	

Friday

8/30/2019

Things to Accomplish

_____

_____

_____

_____

Writing Goals

_____

_____

_____

Rewrite yesterday's exercise in dialogue only.

5:00 AM	
6:00 AM	
7:00 AM	
8:00 AM	
9:00 AM	
10:00 AM	
1:00 AM	
12:00 PM	
1:00 PM	
2:00 PM	
3:00 PM	
4:00 PM	
5:00 PM	
6:00 PM	
7:00 PM	
8:00 PM	
9:00 PM	
10:00 PM	
11:00 PM	

Saturday
8/31/2019

Things to Accomplish

_____

_____

_____

_____

Writing Goals

_____

_____

_____

"Stay positive and happy. Work hard and don't give up hope. Be open to criticism and keep learning. Surround yourself with happy, warm and genuine people."
—Tena Desae

5:00 AM	
6:00 AM	
7:00 AM	
8:00 AM	
9:00 AM	
10:00 AM	
11:00 AM	
12:00 PM	
1:00 PM	
2:00 PM	
3:00 PM	
4:00 PM	
5:00 PM	
6:00 PM	
7:00 PM	
8:00 PM	
9:00 PM	
10:00 PM	
11:00 PM	

Sunday

9/1/2019

Things to Accomplish

_____

_____

_____

_____

Writing Goals

_____

_____

_____

"Yesterday is not ours to recover, but tomorrow is ours to win or lose."
—Lyndon B. Johnson

5:00 AM	
6:00 AM	
7:00 AM	
8:00 AM	
9:00 AM	
10:00 AM	
11:00 AM	
12:00 PM	
1:00 PM	
2:00 PM	
3:00 PM	
4:00 PM	
5:00 PM	
6:00 PM	
7:00 PM	
8:00 PM	
9:00 PM	
10:00 PM	
11:00 PM	

Weekly Planner

_____ to _____

Goals

_____

_____

_____

_____

_____

Notes

MONDAY _____

TUESDAY _____

WEDNESDAY _____

THURSDAY _____

FRIDAY _____

SATURDAY _____

SUNDAY _____

Monday

9/2/2019

Things to Accomplish

_____

_____

_____

_____

Writing Goals

_____

_____

_____

Meditate or sit in silence for 10 minutes to clear your mind. Then reflect on where you are related to your career, relationships, and life in general. Decide which aspect you need to focus on to find balance in your life. Try to find time for this exercise at least once a month.

5:00 AM	
6:00 AM	
7:00 AM	
8:00 AM	
9:00 AM	
10:00 AM	
11:00 AM	
12:00 PM	
1:00 PM	
2:00 PM	
3:00 PM	
4:00 PM	
5:00 PM	
6:00 PM	
7:00 PM	
8:00 PM	
9:00 PM	
10:00 PM	
11:00 PM	

Tuesday

9/3/2019

Things to Accomplish

_____

_____

_____

_____

Writing Goals

_____

_____

_____

"Find a place inside where there's joy, and the joy will burn out the pain."
—Joseph Campbell

5:00 AM	
6:00 AM	
7:00 AM	
8:00 AM	
9:00 AM	
10:00 AM	
11:00 AM	
12:00 PM	
1:00 PM	
2:00 PM	
3:00 PM	
4:00 PM	
5:00 PM	
6:00 PM	
7:00 PM	
8:00 PM	
9:00 PM	
10:00 PM	
11:00 PM	

Wednesday

9/4/2019

Things to Accomplish

_____

_____

_____

_____

Writing Goals

_____

_____

_____

"Creativity is putting your imagination to work, and it's produced the most extraordinary results in human culture."
—Ken Robinson

5:00 AM	
6:00 AM	
7:00 AM	
8:00 AM	
9:00 AM	
10:00 AM	
11:00 AM	
12:00 PM	
1:00 PM	
2:00 PM	
3:00 PM	
4:00 PM	
5:00 PM	
6:00 PM	
7:00 PM	
8:00 PM	
9:00 PM	
10:00 PM	
11:00 PM	

Thursday

9/5/2019

Things to Accomplish

_____

_____

_____

_____

Writing Goals

_____

_____

_____

"You're only given a little
spark of madness. You mustn't
lose it."
—Robin Williams

5:00 AM	
6:00 AM	
7:00 AM	
8:00 AM	
9:00 AM	
10:00 AM	
11:00 AM	
12:00 PM	
1:00 PM	
2:00 PM	
3:00 PM	
4:00 PM	
5:00 PM	
6:00 PM	
7:00 PM	
8:00 PM	
9:00 PM	
10:00 PM	
11:00 PM	

Friday

9/6/2019

Things to Accomplish

_____

_____

_____

_____

Writing Goals

_____

_____

_____

"They who dream by day are cognizant of many things which escape those who dream only by night."
—Edgar Allan Poe

5:00 AM	
6:00 AM	
7:00 AM	
8:00 AM	
9:00 AM	
10:00 AM	
11:00 AM	
12:00 PM	
1:00 PM	
2:00 PM	
3:00 PM	
4:00 PM	
5:00 PM	
6:00 PM	
7:00 PM	
8:00 PM	
9:00 PM	
10:00 PM	
11:00 PM	

Saturday

9/7/2019

Things to Accomplish

_____

_____

_____

_____

Writing Goals

_____

_____

_____

"Change is the end result of all true learning."—Leo Buscaglia

5:00 AM	
6:00 AM	
7:00 AM	
8:00 AM	
9:00 AM	
10:00 AM	
11:00 AM	
12:00 PM	
1:00 PM	
2:00 PM	
3:00 PM	
4:00 PM	
5:00 PM	
6:00 PM	
7:00 PM	
8:00 PM	
9:00 PM	
10:00 PM	
11:00 PM	

Sunday

9/8/2019

Things to Accomplish

_____

_____

_____

Writing Goals

_____

_____

_____

"Progress is impossible
without change, and those
who cannot change their
minds cannot change
anything."
—George Bernard Shaw

5:00 AM	
6:00 AM	
7:00 AM	
8:00 AM	
9:00 AM	
10:00 AM	
11:00 AM	
12:00 PM	
1:00 PM	
2:00 PM	
3:00 PM	
4:00 PM	
5:00 PM	
6:00 PM	
7:00 PM	
8:00 PM	
9:00 PM	
10:00 PM	
11:00 PM	

Weekly Planner

_____ to _____

Goals

_____

_____

_____

_____

_____

Notes

MONDAY _____

TUESDAY _____

WEDNESDAY _____

THURSDAY _____

FRIDAY _____

SATURDAY _____

SUNDAY _____

Monday
9/9/2019

Things to Accomplish

_____

_____

_____

_____

Writing Goals

_____

_____

_____

Crystal Lake Publishing challenge!
Grab a Crystal Lake work and take
a photo of it. Present it like it's
never been photographed before.
Tag us, and we'll send a surprise to
the most unique photo. Twitter:
@crystallakepub Facebook: Crystal
Lake Publishing Instagram:
crystal_lake_publishing

5:00 AM	
6:00 AM	
7:00 AM	
8:00 AM	
9:00 AM	
10:00 AM	
11:00 AM	
12:00 PM	
1:00 PM	
2:00 PM	
3:00 PM	
4:00 PM	
5:00 PM	
6:00 PM	
7:00 PM	
8:00 PM	
9:00 PM	
10:00 PM	
11:00 PM	

Tuesday

9/10/2019

Things to Accomplish

_____

_____

_____

_____

Writing Goals

_____

_____

_____

"A somebody was once a nobody who wanted to and did."—John Burroughs

5:00 AM	
6:00 AM	
7:00 AM	
8:00 AM	
9:00 AM	
10:00 AM	
1:00 AM	
12:00 PM	
1:00 PM	
2:00 PM	
3:00 PM	
4:00 PM	
5:00 PM	
6:00 PM	
7:00 PM	
8:00 PM	
9:00 PM	
10:00 PM	
11:00 PM	

Wednesday
9/11/2019

Things to Accomplish

_____

_____

_____

Writing Goals

_____

_____

_____

"If you fell down yesterday, stand up today."—H. G. Wells

5:00 AM	
6:00 AM	
7:00 AM	
8:00 AM	
9:00 AM	
10:00 AM	
11:00 AM	
12:00 PM	
1:00 PM	
2:00 PM	
3:00 PM	
4:00 PM	
5:00 PM	
6:00 PM	
7:00 PM	
8:00 PM	
9:00 PM	
10:00 PM	
11:00 PM	

Thursday
9/12/2019

Things to Accomplish

_____

_____

_____

_____

Writing Goals

_____

_____

_____

"Our greatest weakness lies in giving up. The most certain way to succeed is always to try just one more time."
—Thomas A. Edison

5:00 AM	
6:00 AM	
7:00 AM	
8:00 AM	
9:00 AM	
10:00 AM	
11:00 AM	
12:00 PM	
1:00 PM	
2:00 PM	
3:00 PM	
4:00 PM	
5:00 PM	
6:00 PM	
7:00 PM	
8:00 PM	
9:00 PM	
10:00 PM	
11:00 PM	

Friday

9/13/2019

Things to Accomplish

_____

_____

_____

_____

Writing Goals

_____

_____

_____

"Setting goals is the first step in turning the invisible into the visible."—Tony Robbins

5:00 AM	
6:00 AM	
7:00 AM	
8:00 AM	
9:00 AM	
10:00 AM	
11:00 AM	
12:00 PM	
1:00 PM	
2:00 PM	
3:00 PM	
4:00 PM	
5:00 PM	
6:00 PM	
7:00 PM	
8:00 PM	
9:00 PM	
10:00 PM	
11:00 PM	

Saturday

9/14/2019

Things to Accomplish

_____

_____

_____

_____

Writing Goals

_____

_____

_____

"Quality is not an act, it is a
habit."—Aristotle

5:00 AM	
6:00 AM	
7:00 AM	
8:00 AM	
9:00 AM	
10:00 AM	
11:00 AM	
12:00 PM	
1:00 PM	
2:00 PM	
3:00 PM	
4:00 PM	
5:00 PM	
6:00 PM	
7:00 PM	
8:00 PM	
9:00 PM	
10:00 PM	
11:00 PM	

Sunday

9/15/2019

Things to Accomplish

_____

_____

_____

_____

Writing Goals

_____

_____

_____

"We may encounter many
defeats but we must not be
defeated."—Maya Angelou

5:00 AM	
6:00 AM	
7:00 AM	
8:00 AM	
9:00 AM	
10:00 AM	
11:00 AM	
12:00 PM	
1:00 PM	
2:00 PM	
3:00 PM	
4:00 PM	
5:00 PM	
6:00 PM	
7:00 PM	
8:00 PM	
9:00 PM	
10:00 PM	
11:00 PM	

Weekly Planner

_____ to _____

Goals

_____

_____

_____

_____

_____

Notes

MONDAY _____

TUESDAY _____

WEDNESDAY _____

THURSDAY _____

FRIDAY _____

SATURDAY _____

SUNDAY _____

Monday

9/16/2019

Things to Accomplish

_____

_____

_____

_____

Writing Goals

_____

_____

_____

"The future belongs to those who believe in the beauty of their dreams."
—Eleanor Roosevelt

5:00 AM	
6:00 AM	
7:00 AM	
8:00 AM	
9:00 AM	
10:00 AM	
11:00 AM	
12:00 PM	
1:00 PM	
2:00 PM	
3:00 PM	
4:00 PM	
5:00 PM	
6:00 PM	
7:00 PM	
8:00 PM	
9:00 PM	
10:00 PM	
11:00 PM	

Tuesday

9/17/2019

Things to Accomplish

_____

_____

_____

_____

Writing Goals

_____

_____

_____

"Action is the foundational key
to all success."
—Pablo Picasso

5:00 AM	
6:00 AM	
7:00 AM	
8:00 AM	
9:00 AM	
10:00 AM	
1:00 AM	
12:00 PM	
1:00 PM	
2:00 PM	
3:00 PM	
4:00 PM	
5:00 PM	
6:00 PM	
7:00 PM	
8:00 PM	
9:00 PM	
10:00 PM	
11:00 PM	

Wednesday

9/18/2019

Things to Accomplish

_____

_____

_____

_____

Writing Goals

_____

_____

_____

Grab a book written in the 1900s and rewrite a page in your own voice and style, focusing on using more showing than telling (which was quite popular back then).

5:00 AM
6:00 AM
7:00 AM
8:00 AM
9:00 AM
10:00 AM
1:00 AM
12:00 PM
1:00 PM
2:00 PM
3:00 PM
4:00 PM
5:00 PM
6:00 PM
7:00 PM
8:00 PM
9:00 PM
10:00 PM
11:00 PM

Thursday

9/19/2019

Things to Accomplish

_____

_____

_____

_____

Writing Goals

_____

_____

_____

"You have to make it happen."—Denis Diderot

5:00 AM	
6:00 AM	
7:00 AM	
8:00 AM	
9:00 AM	
10:00 AM	
1:00 AM	
12:00 PM	
1:00 PM	
2:00 PM	
3:00 PM	
4:00 PM	
5:00 PM	
6:00 PM	
7:00 PM	
8:00 PM	
9:00 PM	
10:00 PM	
11:00 PM	

Friday

9/20/2019

Things to Accomplish

_____

_____

_____

_____

Writing Goals

_____

_____

_____

"You are never too old to set another goal or to dream a new dream."—Les Brown

5:00 AM	
6:00 AM	
7:00 AM	
8:00 AM	
9:00 AM	
10:00 AM	
11:00 AM	
12:00 PM	
1:00 PM	
2:00 PM	
3:00 PM	
4:00 PM	
5:00 PM	
6:00 PM	
7:00 PM	
8:00 PM	
9:00 PM	
10:00 PM	
11:00 PM	

Saturday

9/21/2019

Things to Accomplish

_____

_____

_____

_____

Writing Goals

_____

_____

_____

"Things do not happen. Things
are made to happen."
—John F. Kennedy

5:00 AM	
6:00 AM	
7:00 AM	
8:00 AM	
9:00 AM	
10:00 AM	
11:00 AM	
12:00 PM	
1:00 PM	
2:00 PM	
3:00 PM	
4:00 PM	
5:00 PM	
6:00 PM	
7:00 PM	
8:00 PM	
9:00 PM	
10:00 PM	
11:00 PM	

Sunday

9/22/2019

Things to Accomplish

_____

_____

_____

_____

Writing Goals

_____

_____

_____

"Be miserable. Or motivate yourself. Whatever has to be done, it's always your choice."—Wayne Dyer

5:00 AM	
6:00 AM	
7:00 AM	
8:00 AM	
9:00 AM	
10:00 AM	
11:00 AM	
12:00 PM	
1:00 PM	
2:00 PM	
3:00 PM	
4:00 PM	
5:00 PM	
6:00 PM	
7:00 PM	
8:00 PM	
9:00 PM	
10:00 PM	
11:00 PM	

Weekly Planner

_____ to _____

Goals

_____

_____

_____

_____

_____

Notes

MONDAY _____

TUESDAY _____

WEDNESDAY _____

THURSDAY _____

FRIDAY _____

SATURDAY _____

SUNDAY _____

Monday
9/23/2019

Things to Accomplish

_____

_____

_____

_____

Writing Goals

_____

_____

_____

"Never give up, for that is just
the place and time that the
tide will turn."
—Harriet Beecher Stowe

5:00 AM	
6:00 AM	
7:00 AM	
8:00 AM	
9:00 AM	
10:00 AM	
11:00 AM	
12:00 PM	
1:00 PM	
2:00 PM	
3:00 PM	
4:00 PM	
5:00 PM	
6:00 PM	
7:00 PM	
8:00 PM	
9:00 PM	
10:00 PM	
11:00 PM	

Tuesday
9/24/2019

Things to Accomplish

_____

_____

_____

_____

Writing Goals

_____

_____

_____

"When you reach the end of
your rope, tie a knot in it and
hang on."
—Franklin D. Roosevelt

5:00 AM	
6:00 AM	
7:00 AM	
8:00 AM	
9:00 AM	
10:00 AM	
11:00 AM	
12:00 PM	
1:00 PM	
2:00 PM	
3:00 PM	
4:00 PM	
5:00 PM	
6:00 PM	
7:00 PM	
8:00 PM	
9:00 PM	
10:00 PM	
11:00 PM	

Wednesday

9/25/2019

Things to Accomplish

_____

_____

_____

_____

Writing Goals

_____

_____

_____

Crystal Lake Publishing challenge!
Use social media to tell people
outside your town/city/area about a
local legend or true story—be it
humorous, tragic, etc. Be sure to tag
us: Twitter: @crystallakepub
Facebook: Crystal Lake Publishing

5:00 AM	
6:00 AM	
7:00 AM	
8:00 AM	
9:00 AM	
10:00 AM	
11:00 AM	
12:00 PM	
1:00 PM	
2:00 PM	
3:00 PM	
4:00 PM	
5:00 PM	
6:00 PM	
7:00 PM	
8:00 PM	
9:00 PM	
10:00 PM	
11:00 PM	

Thursday
9/26/2019

Things to Accomplish

_____

_____

_____

_____

Writing Goals

_____

_____

_____

"No matter what people tell you, words and ideas can change the world."
—Robin Williams

5:00 AM	
6:00 AM	
7:00 AM	
8:00 AM	
9:00 AM	
10:00 AM	
11:00 AM	
12:00 PM	
1:00 PM	
2:00 PM	
3:00 PM	
4:00 PM	
5:00 PM	
6:00 PM	
7:00 PM	
8:00 PM	
9:00 PM	
10:00 PM	
11:00 PM	

Friday
9/27/2019
Things to Accomplish

_____

_____

_____

Writing Goals

_____

_____

_____

Take your imagination with you today. Concentrate on seeing everything in a way they've never been. Give life to the clouds, eyes to the buildings, thoughts to objects.

5:00 AM	
6:00 AM	
7:00 AM	
8:00 AM	
9:00 AM	
10:00 AM	
11:00 AM	
12:00 PM	
1:00 PM	
2:00 PM	
3:00 PM	
4:00 PM	
5:00 PM	
6:00 PM	
7:00 PM	
8:00 PM	
9:00 PM	
10:00 PM	
11:00 PM	

Saturday

9/28/2019

Things to Accomplish

_____

_____

_____

_____

Writing Goals

_____

_____

_____

Visualize your favorite fantasy world, be it The Shire, Hogwarts, Amity, Gotham City, or even King's Landing. Describe what you'd see outside your window.

5:00 AM	
6:00 AM	
7:00 AM	
8:00 AM	
9:00 AM	
10:00 AM	
11:00 AM	
12:00 PM	
1:00 PM	
2:00 PM	
3:00 PM	
4:00 PM	
5:00 PM	
6:00 PM	
7:00 PM	
8:00 PM	
9:00 PM	
10:00 PM	
11:00 PM	

Sunday
9/29/2019

Things to Accomplish

_____

_____

_____

_____

Writing Goals

_____

_____

_____

"If there is no struggle, there
is no progress."
—Frederick Douglass

5:00 AM	
6:00 AM	
7:00 AM	
8:00 AM	
9:00 AM	
10:00 AM	
11:00 AM	
12:00 PM	
1:00 PM	
2:00 PM	
3:00 PM	
4:00 PM	
5:00 PM	
6:00 PM	
7:00 PM	
8:00 PM	
9:00 PM	
10:00 PM	
11:00 PM	

Weekly Planner

_____ to _____

Goals

_____

_____

_____

_____

_____

Notes

MONDAY _____

TUESDAY _____

WEDNESDAY _____

THURSDAY _____

FRIDAY _____

SATURDAY _____

SUNDAY _____

Monday

9/30/2019

Things to Accomplish

_____

_____

_____

_____

Writing Goals

_____

_____

_____

Without changing your daily routine of visiting any new places, consciously try to see things you tend to miss on a daily basis. Experience the finer details of your surroundings and the objects that fill it.

5:00 AM	
6:00 AM	
7:00 AM	
8:00 AM	
9:00 AM	
10:00 AM	
11:00 AM	
12:00 PM	
1:00 PM	
2:00 PM	
3:00 PM	
4:00 PM	
5:00 PM	
6:00 PM	
7:00 PM	
8:00 PM	
9:00 PM	
10:00 PM	
11:00 PM	

Tuesday
10/1/2019

Things to Accomplish

_____

_____

_____

_____

Writing Goals

_____

_____

_____

"Growth is painful. Change is
painful. But, nothing is as
painful as staying stuck where
you do not belong."
—N. R. Narayana Murthy

5:00 AM	
6:00 AM	
7:00 AM	
8:00 AM	
9:00 AM	
10:00 AM	
1:00 AM	
12:00 PM	
1:00 PM	
2:00 PM	
3:00 PM	
4:00 PM	
5:00 PM	
6:00 PM	
7:00 PM	
8:00 PM	
9:00 PM	
10:00 PM	
11:00 PM	

Wednesday

10/2/2019

Things to Accomplish

_____

_____

_____

_____

Writing Goals

_____

_____

_____

"For success, attitude is equally as important as ability."—Walter Scott

5:00 AM	
6:00 AM	
7:00 AM	
8:00 AM	
9:00 AM	
10:00 AM	
11:00 AM	
12:00 PM	
1:00 PM	
2:00 PM	
3:00 PM	
4:00 PM	
5:00 PM	
6:00 PM	
7:00 PM	
8:00 PM	
9:00 PM	
10:00 PM	
11:00 PM	

Thursday

10/3/2019

Things to Accomplish

_____

_____

_____

_____

Writing Goals

_____

_____

_____

Compile a list of objects you'd expect on your work-in-progress' character's (or a recent character you created) nightstand.

5:00 AM	
6:00 AM	
7:00 AM	
8:00 AM	
9:00 AM	
10:00 AM	
11:00 AM	
12:00 PM	
1:00 PM	
2:00 PM	
3:00 PM	
4:00 PM	
5:00 PM	
6:00 PM	
7:00 PM	
8:00 PM	
9:00 PM	
10:00 PM	
11:00 PM	

Friday

10/4/2019

Things to Accomplish

_____

_____

_____

_____

Writing Goals

_____

_____

_____

"Weakness of attitude
becomes weakness of
character."—Albert Einstein

5:00 AM	
6:00 AM	
7:00 AM	
8:00 AM	
9:00 AM	
10:00 AM	
11:00 AM	
12:00 PM	
1:00 PM	
2:00 PM	
3:00 PM	
4:00 PM	
5:00 PM	
6:00 PM	
7:00 PM	
8:00 PM	
9:00 PM	
10:00 PM	
11:00 PM	

Saturday
10/5/2019

Things to Accomplish

_____

_____

_____

_____

Writing Goals

_____

_____

_____

"If you have a positive attitude and constantly strive to give your best effort, eventually you will overcome your immediate problems and find you are ready for greater challenges."—Pat Riley

5:00 AM	
6:00 AM	
7:00 AM	
8:00 AM	
9:00 AM	
10:00 AM	
11:00 AM	
12:00 PM	
1:00 PM	
2:00 PM	
3:00 PM	
4:00 PM	
5:00 PM	
6:00 PM	
7:00 PM	
8:00 PM	
9:00 PM	
10:00 PM	
11:00 PM	

Sunday

10/6/2019

Things to Accomplish

_____

_____

_____

_____

Writing Goals

_____

_____

_____

Ability is what you're capable of doing. Motivation determines what you do. Attitude determines how well you do it. —Lou Holtz

5:00 AM	
6:00 AM	
7:00 AM	
8:00 AM	
9:00 AM	
10:00 AM	
11:00 AM	
12:00 PM	
1:00 PM	
2:00 PM	
3:00 PM	
4:00 PM	
5:00 PM	
6:00 PM	
7:00 PM	
8:00 PM	
9:00 PM	
10:00 PM	
11:00 PM	

Weekly Planner

_____ to _____

Goals

_____

_____

_____

_____

_____

Notes

MONDAY _____

TUESDAY _____

WEDNESDAY _____

THURSDAY _____

FRIDAY _____

SATURDAY _____

SUNDAY _____

Monday

10/7/2019

Things to Accomplish

_____

_____

_____

_____

Writing Goals

_____

_____

_____

"If you are going to achieve excellence in big things, you develop the habit in little matters. Excellence is not an exception, it is a prevailing attitude."—Colin Powell

5:00 AM
6:00 AM
7:00 AM
8:00 AM
9:00 AM
10:00 AM
11:00 AM
12:00 PM
1:00 PM
2:00 PM
3:00 PM
4:00 PM
5:00 PM
6:00 PM
7:00 PM
8:00 PM
9:00 PM
10:00 PM
11:00 PM

Tuesday

10/8/2019

Things to Accomplish

_____

_____

_____

_____

Writing Goals

_____

_____

_____

"Knowledge will give you power, but character respect."—Bruce Lee

5:00 AM	
6:00 AM	
7:00 AM	
8:00 AM	
9:00 AM	
10:00 AM	
11:00 AM	
12:00 PM	
1:00 PM	
2:00 PM	
3:00 PM	
4:00 PM	
5:00 PM	
6:00 PM	
7:00 PM	
8:00 PM	
9:00 PM	
10:00 PM	
11:00 PM	

Wednesday

10/9/2019

Things to Accomplish

_____

_____

_____

_____

Writing Goals

_____

_____

_____

"You will never change your
life until you change
something you do daily."
—Mike Murdock

5:00 AM	
6:00 AM	
7:00 AM	
8:00 AM	
9:00 AM	
10:00 AM	
11:00 AM	
12:00 PM	
1:00 PM	
2:00 PM	
3:00 PM	
4:00 PM	
5:00 PM	
6:00 PM	
7:00 PM	
8:00 PM	
9:00 PM	
10:00 PM	
11:00 PM	

Thursday

10/10/2019

Things to Accomplish

_____

_____

_____

_____

Writing Goals

_____

_____

_____

"Some days are just bad days, that's all. You have to experience sadness to know happiness, and I remind myself that not every day is going to be a good day, that's just the way it is!"—Dita Von Teese

5:00 AM	
6:00 AM	
7:00 AM	
8:00 AM	
9:00 AM	
10:00 AM	
11:00 AM	
12:00 PM	
1:00 PM	
2:00 PM	
3:00 PM	
4:00 PM	
5:00 PM	
6:00 PM	
7:00 PM	
8:00 PM	
9:00 PM	
10:00 PM	
11:00 PM	

Friday

10/11/2019

Things to Accomplish

_____

_____

_____

_____

Writing Goals

_____

_____

_____

Write a letter to your emotional/hormonal high school self.

5:00 AM	
6:00 AM	
7:00 AM	
8:00 AM	
9:00 AM	
10:00 AM	
11:00 AM	
12:00 PM	
1:00 PM	
2:00 PM	
3:00 PM	
4:00 PM	
5:00 PM	
6:00 PM	
7:00 PM	
8:00 PM	
9:00 PM	
10:00 PM	
11:00 PM	

Saturday

10/12/2019

Things to Accomplish

_____

_____

_____

_____

Writing Goals

_____

_____

_____

"Always do your best. What you plant now, you will harvest later."—Og Mandino

5:00 AM	
6:00 AM	
7:00 AM	
8:00 AM	
9:00 AM	
10:00 AM	
11:00 AM	
12:00 PM	
1:00 PM	
2:00 PM	
3:00 PM	
4:00 PM	
5:00 PM	
6:00 PM	
7:00 PM	
8:00 PM	
9:00 PM	
10:00 PM	
11:00 PM	

Sunday
10/13/2019

Things to Accomplish

_____

_____

_____

_____

Writing Goals

_____

_____

_____

"Problems are not stop signs,
they are guidelines."
—Robert H. Schuller

5:00 AM	
6:00 AM	
7:00 AM	
8:00 AM	
9:00 AM	
10:00 AM	
1:00 AM	
12:00 PM	
1:00 PM	
2:00 PM	
3:00 PM	
4:00 PM	
5:00 PM	
6:00 PM	
7:00 PM	
8:00 PM	
9:00 PM	
10:00 PM	
11:00 PM	

Weekly Planner

_____ to _____

Goals

_____

_____

_____

_____

Notes

MONDAY _____

TUESDAY _____

WEDNESDAY _____

THURSDAY _____

FRIDAY _____

SATURDAY _____

SUNDAY _____

Monday

10/14/2019

Things to Accomplish

_____

_____

_____

_____

Writing Goals

_____

_____

_____

"Without hard work, nothing
grows but weeds."
—Gordon B. Hinckley

5:00 AM	
6:00 AM	
7:00 AM	
8:00 AM	
9:00 AM	
10:00 AM	
11:00 AM	
12:00 PM	
1:00 PM	
2:00 PM	
3:00 PM	
4:00 PM	
5:00 PM	
6:00 PM	
7:00 PM	
8:00 PM	
9:00 PM	
10:00 PM	
11:00 PM	

Tuesday
10/15/2019

Things to Accomplish

_____

_____

_____

_____

Writing Goals

_____

_____

_____

"If you can dream it, you can do it."—Walt Disney

5:00 AM	
6:00 AM	
7:00 AM	
8:00 AM	
9:00 AM	
10:00 AM	
11:00 AM	
12:00 PM	
1:00 PM	
2:00 PM	
3:00 PM	
4:00 PM	
5:00 PM	
6:00 PM	
7:00 PM	
8:00 PM	
9:00 PM	
10:00 PM	
11:00 PM	

Wednesday

10/16/2019

Things to Accomplish

_____

_____

_____

_____

Writing Goals

_____

_____

_____

"If you want to conquer fear,
don't sit home and think
about it. Go out and get busy."
—Dale Carnegie

5:00 AM	
6:00 AM	
7:00 AM	
8:00 AM	
9:00 AM	
10:00 AM	
11:00 AM	
12:00 PM	
1:00 PM	
2:00 PM	
3:00 PM	
4:00 PM	
5:00 PM	
6:00 PM	
7:00 PM	
8:00 PM	
9:00 PM	
10:00 PM	
11:00 PM	

Thursday

10/17/2019

Things to Accomplish

_____

_____

_____

Writing Goals

_____

_____

_____

"There is only one corner of
the universe you can be
certain of improving, and
that's your own self."
—Aldous Huxley

5:00 AM	
6:00 AM	
7:00 AM	
8:00 AM	
9:00 AM	
10:00 AM	
11:00 AM	
12:00 PM	
1:00 PM	
2:00 PM	
3:00 PM	
4:00 PM	
5:00 PM	
6:00 PM	
7:00 PM	
8:00 PM	
9:00 PM	
10:00 PM	
11:00 PM	

Friday

10/18/2019

Things to Accomplish

_____

_____

_____

_____

Writing Goals

_____

_____

_____

"You gain strength, courage, and confidence by every experience in which you really stop to look fear in the face. You are able to say to yourself, 'I lived through this horror. I can take the next thing that comes along."
—Eleanor Roosevelt

5:00 AM	
6:00 AM	
7:00 AM	
8:00 AM	
9:00 AM	
10:00 AM	
11:00 AM	
12:00 PM	
1:00 PM	
2:00 PM	
3:00 PM	
4:00 PM	
5:00 PM	
6:00 PM	
7:00 PM	
8:00 PM	
9:00 PM	
10:00 PM	
11:00 PM	

Saturday

10/19/2019

Things to Accomplish

_____

_____

_____

_____

Writing Goals

_____

_____

_____

"Character cannot be developed in ease and quiet. Only through experience of trial and suffering can the soul be strengthened, ambition inspired, and success achieved."—Helen Keller

5:00 AM	
6:00 AM	
7:00 AM	
8:00 AM	
9:00 AM	
10:00 AM	
11:00 AM	
12:00 PM	
1:00 PM	
2:00 PM	
3:00 PM	
4:00 PM	
5:00 PM	
6:00 PM	
7:00 PM	
8:00 PM	
9:00 PM	
10:00 PM	
11:00 PM	

Sunday

10/20/2019

Things to Accomplish

_____

_____

_____

_____

Writing Goals

_____

_____

_____

"I believe that imagination is stronger than knowledge. That myth is more potent than history. That dreams are more powerful than facts."
—Robert Fulghum

5:00 AM	
6:00 AM	
7:00 AM	
8:00 AM	
9:00 AM	
10:00 AM	
11:00 AM	
12:00 PM	
1:00 PM	
2:00 PM	
3:00 PM	
4:00 PM	
5:00 PM	
6:00 PM	
7:00 PM	
8:00 PM	
9:00 PM	
10:00 PM	
11:00 PM	

Weekly Planner

_____ to _____

Goals

_____

_____

_____

_____

_____

Notes

MONDAY _____

TUESDAY _____

WEDNESDAY _____

THURSDAY _____

FRIDAY _____

SATURDAY _____

SUNDAY _____

Monday
10/21/2019

Things to Accomplish

_____

_____

_____

_____

Writing Goals

_____

_____

_____

Use today to ask a friend or acquaintance about an interesting story from their life. Use this reconnect with your passion for stories.

5:00 AM	
6:00 AM	
7:00 AM	
8:00 AM	
9:00 AM	
10:00 AM	
11:00 AM	
12:00 PM	
1:00 PM	
2:00 PM	
3:00 PM	
4:00 PM	
5:00 PM	
6:00 PM	
7:00 PM	
8:00 PM	
9:00 PM	
10:00 PM	
11:00 PM	

Tuesday

10/22/2019

Things to Accomplish

_____

_____

_____

_____

Writing Goals

_____

_____

_____

"Be brave. Take risks. Nothing
can substitute experience."
—Paulo Coelho

5:00 AM	
6:00 AM	
7:00 AM	
8:00 AM	
9:00 AM	
10:00 AM	
11:00 AM	
12:00 PM	
1:00 PM	
2:00 PM	
3:00 PM	
4:00 PM	
5:00 PM	
6:00 PM	
7:00 PM	
8:00 PM	
9:00 PM	
10:00 PM	
11:00 PM	

Wednesday
10/23/2019

Things to Accomplish

_____

_____

_____

_____

Writing Goals

_____

_____

_____

"Life is the art of drawing
without an eraser."
—John W. Gardner

5:00 AM	
6:00 AM	
7:00 AM	
8:00 AM	
9:00 AM	
10:00 AM	
11:00 AM	
12:00 PM	
1:00 PM	
2:00 PM	
3:00 PM	
4:00 PM	
5:00 PM	
6:00 PM	
7:00 PM	
8:00 PM	
9:00 PM	
10:00 PM	
11:00 PM	

Thursday
10/24/2019

Things to Accomplish

_____

_____

_____

Writing Goals

_____

_____

_____

"The only source of knowledge
is experience."
—Albert Einstein

5:00 AM	
6:00 AM	
7:00 AM	
8:00 AM	
9:00 AM	
10:00 AM	
1:00 AM	
12:00 PM	
1:00 PM	
2:00 PM	
3:00 PM	
4:00 PM	
5:00 PM	
6:00 PM	
7:00 PM	
8:00 PM	
9:00 PM	
10:00 PM	
11:00 PM	

Friday

10/25/2019

Things to Accomplish

_____

_____

_____

_____

Writing Goals

_____

_____

_____

Read a scene from a random book and draw (yes, draw) a sketch of the vision you saw, using your imagination to fill in all the blanks. Go big with the details. Your imagination can make the impossible happen, so don't hold back. Anything goes.

5:00 AM	
6:00 AM	
7:00 AM	
8:00 AM	
9:00 AM	
10:00 AM	
11:00 AM	
12:00 PM	
1:00 PM	
2:00 PM	
3:00 PM	
4:00 PM	
5:00 PM	
6:00 PM	
7:00 PM	
8:00 PM	
9:00 PM	
10:00 PM	
11:00 PM	

Saturday

10/26/2019

Things to Accomplish

_____

_____

_____

_____

Writing Goals

_____

_____

_____

"Only I can change my life. No one can do it for me."
—Carol Burnett

5:00 AM	
6:00 AM	
7:00 AM	
8:00 AM	
9:00 AM	
10:00 AM	
11:00 AM	
12:00 PM	
1:00 PM	
2:00 PM	
3:00 PM	
4:00 PM	
5:00 PM	
6:00 PM	
7:00 PM	
8:00 PM	
9:00 PM	
10:00 PM	
11:00 PM	

Sunday
10/27/2019

Things to Accomplish

_____

_____

_____

_____

Writing Goals

_____

_____

_____

"With the new day comes new strength and new thoughts."
—Eleanor Roosevelt

5:00 AM	
6:00 AM	
7:00 AM	
8:00 AM	
9:00 AM	
10:00 AM	
11:00 AM	
12:00 PM	
1:00 PM	
2:00 PM	
3:00 PM	
4:00 PM	
5:00 PM	
6:00 PM	
7:00 PM	
8:00 PM	
9:00 PM	
10:00 PM	
11:00 PM	

Weekly Planner

_____ to _____

Goals

_____

_____

_____

_____

Notes

MONDAY _____

TUESDAY _____

WEDNESDAY _____

THURSDAY _____

FRIDAY _____

SATURDAY _____

SUNDAY _____

Monday
10/28/2019

Things to Accomplish

_____

_____

_____

_____

Writing Goals

_____

_____

_____

"Failure will never overtake
me if my determination to
succeed is strong enough."
—Og Mandino

5:00 AM	
6:00 AM	
7:00 AM	
8:00 AM	
9:00 AM	
10:00 AM	
11:00 AM	
12:00 PM	
1:00 PM	
2:00 PM	
3:00 PM	
4:00 PM	
5:00 PM	
6:00 PM	
7:00 PM	
8:00 PM	
9:00 PM	
10:00 PM	
11:00 PM	

Tuesday
10/29/2019

Things to Accomplish

_____

_____

_____

_____

Writing Goals

_____

_____

_____

"Change your life today. Don't gamble on the future, act now, without delay."
—Simone de Beauvoir

5:00 AM	
6:00 AM	
7:00 AM	
8:00 AM	
9:00 AM	
10:00 AM	
1:00 AM	
12:00 PM	
1:00 PM	
2:00 PM	
3:00 PM	
4:00 PM	
5:00 PM	
6:00 PM	
7:00 PM	
8:00 PM	
9:00 PM	
10:00 PM	
11:00 PM	

Wednesday
10/30/2019
Things to Accomplish

_____

_____

_____

_____

Writing Goals

_____

_____

_____

"Act as if what you do makes a difference. It does."
—William James

5:00 AM	
6:00 AM	
7:00 AM	
8:00 AM	
9:00 AM	
10:00 AM	
1:00 AM	
12:00 PM	
1:00 PM	
2:00 PM	
3:00 PM	
4:00 PM	
5:00 PM	
6:00 PM	
7:00 PM	
8:00 PM	
9:00 PM	
10:00 PM	
11:00 PM	

Thursday
10/31/2019

Things to Accomplish

_____

_____

_____

_____

Writing Goals

_____

_____

_____

"We should not give up and we
should not allow the problem
to defeat us."
—A. P. J. Abdul Kalam

5:00 AM	
6:00 AM	
7:00 AM	
8:00 AM	
9:00 AM	
10:00 AM	
11:00 AM	
12:00 PM	
1:00 PM	
2:00 PM	
3:00 PM	
4:00 PM	
5:00 PM	
6:00 PM	
7:00 PM	
8:00 PM	
9:00 PM	
10:00 PM	
11:00 PM	

Friday

11/1/2019

Things to Accomplish

_____

_____

_____

_____

Writing Goals

_____

_____

_____

"You can't cross the sea merely by standing and staring at the water."
—Rabindranath Tagore

5:00 AM	
6:00 AM	
7:00 AM	
8:00 AM	
9:00 AM	
10:00 AM	
11:00 AM	
12:00 PM	
1:00 PM	
2:00 PM	
3:00 PM	
4:00 PM	
5:00 PM	
6:00 PM	
7:00 PM	
8:00 PM	
9:00 PM	
10:00 PM	
11:00 PM	

Saturday

11/2/2019

Things to Accomplish

_____

_____

_____

_____

Writing Goals

_____

_____

_____

"The reward of suffering is experience."
—Harry S Truman

5:00 AM	
6:00 AM	
7:00 AM	
8:00 AM	
9:00 AM	
10:00 AM	
1:00 AM	
12:00 PM	
1:00 PM	
2:00 PM	
3:00 PM	
4:00 PM	
5:00 PM	
6:00 PM	
7:00 PM	
8:00 PM	
9:00 PM	
10:00 PM	
11:00 PM	

Sunday

11/3/2019

Things to Accomplish

_____

_____

_____

_____

Writing Goals

_____

_____

_____

"Experience is a hard teacher
because she gives the test first,
the lesson afterward."
—Vernon Law

5:00 AM	
6:00 AM	
7:00 AM	
8:00 AM	
9:00 AM	
10:00 AM	
11:00 AM	
12:00 PM	
1:00 PM	
2:00 PM	
3:00 PM	
4:00 PM	
5:00 PM	
6:00 PM	
7:00 PM	
8:00 PM	
9:00 PM	
10:00 PM	
11:00 PM	

Weekly Planner

_____ to _____

Goals

_____

_____

_____

_____

_____

Notes

MONDAY _____

TUESDAY _____

WEDNESDAY _____

THURSDAY _____

FRIDAY _____

SATURDAY _____

SUNDAY _____

Monday
11/4/2019

Things to Accomplish

_____

_____

_____

_____

Writing Goals

_____

_____

_____

"The most beautiful thing we can experience is the mysterious. It is the source of all true art and science."
—Albert Einstein

5:00 AM	
6:00 AM	
7:00 AM	
8:00 AM	
9:00 AM	
10:00 AM	
11:00 AM	
12:00 PM	
1:00 PM	
2:00 PM	
3:00 PM	
4:00 PM	
5:00 PM	
6:00 PM	
7:00 PM	
8:00 PM	
9:00 PM	
10:00 PM	
11:00 PM	

Tuesday
11/5/2019

Things to Accomplish

_____

_____

_____

_____

Writing Goals

_____

_____

_____

Crystal Lake Publishing challenge!
Support a small or 2nd hand
bookstore this week. Share a photo
on social media and be sure to tag
us: Twitter: @crystallakepub
Facebook: Crystal Lake Publishing
Instagram: crystal_lake_publishing

5:00 AM	
6:00 AM	
7:00 AM	
8:00 AM	
9:00 AM	
10:00 AM	
11:00 AM	
12:00 PM	
1:00 PM	
2:00 PM	
3:00 PM	
4:00 PM	
5:00 PM	
6:00 PM	
7:00 PM	
8:00 PM	
9:00 PM	
10:00 PM	
11:00 PM	

Wednesday

11/6/2019

Things to Accomplish

_____

_____

_____

_____

Writing Goals

_____

_____

_____

"Experience is not what
happens to you; it's what you
do with what happens to
you."—Aldous Huxley

5:00 AM	
6:00 AM	
7:00 AM	
8:00 AM	
9:00 AM	
10:00 AM	
11:00 AM	
12:00 PM	
1:00 PM	
2:00 PM	
3:00 PM	
4:00 PM	
5:00 PM	
6:00 PM	
7:00 PM	
8:00 PM	
9:00 PM	
10:00 PM	
11:00 PM	

Thursday
11/7/2019

Things to Accomplish

_____

_____

_____

_____

Writing Goals

_____

_____

_____

"Security is mostly a superstition. It does not exist in nature, nor do the children of men as a whole experience it. Avoiding danger is no safer in the long run than outright exposure. Life is either a daring adventure, or nothing."
—Helen Keller

5:00 AM	
6:00 AM	
7:00 AM	
8:00 AM	
9:00 AM	
10:00 AM	
11:00 AM	
12:00 PM	
1:00 PM	
2:00 PM	
3:00 PM	
4:00 PM	
5:00 PM	
6:00 PM	
7:00 PM	
8:00 PM	
9:00 PM	
10:00 PM	
11:00 PM	

Friday

11/8/2019

Things to Accomplish

_____

_____

_____

_____

Writing Goals

_____

_____

_____

"The soul should always stand
ajar, ready to welcome the
ecstatic experience."
—Emily Dickinson

5:00 AM	
6:00 AM	
7:00 AM	
8:00 AM	
9:00 AM	
10:00 AM	
11:00 AM	
12:00 PM	
1:00 PM	
2:00 PM	
3:00 PM	
4:00 PM	
5:00 PM	
6:00 PM	
7:00 PM	
8:00 PM	
9:00 PM	
10:00 PM	
11:00 PM	

Saturday

11/9/2019

Things to Accomplish

_____

_____

_____

_____

Writing Goals

_____

_____

_____

"The true mark of professionalism is the ability to respect everyone else for their styles and always find something positive in every dining experience and highlight it in your thoughts and words."—Johnny Iuzzini

5:00 AM	
6:00 AM	
7:00 AM	
8:00 AM	
9:00 AM	
10:00 AM	
11:00 AM	
12:00 PM	
1:00 PM	
2:00 PM	
3:00 PM	
4:00 PM	
5:00 PM	
6:00 PM	
7:00 PM	
8:00 PM	
9:00 PM	
10:00 PM	
11:00 PM	

Sunday

11/10/2019

Things to Accomplish

_____

_____

_____

_____

Writing Goals

_____

_____

_____

"Your writing is a representation of who you are. Educate yourself and your emotions, and you'll improve your writing."—Joe Mynhardt

5:00 AM	
6:00 AM	
7:00 AM	
8:00 AM	
9:00 AM	
10:00 AM	
11:00 AM	
12:00 PM	
1:00 PM	
2:00 PM	
3:00 PM	
4:00 PM	
5:00 PM	
6:00 PM	
7:00 PM	
8:00 PM	
9:00 PM	
10:00 PM	
11:00 PM	

Weekly Planner

_____ to _____

Goals

_____

_____

_____

_____

Notes

MONDAY _____

TUESDAY _____

WEDNESDAY _____

THURSDAY _____

FRIDAY _____

SATURDAY _____

SUNDAY _____

Monday
11/11/2019

Things to Accomplish

_____

_____

_____

_____

Writing Goals

_____

_____

_____

"Try to come up with 25 ways to describe something. Start simple and get progressively more outrageous. It's a simple game but great for freeing up a stuck imagination.
—Paul F. Olson

5:00 AM	
6:00 AM	
7:00 AM	
8:00 AM	
9:00 AM	
10:00 AM	
11:00 AM	
12:00 PM	
1:00 PM	
2:00 PM	
3:00 PM	
4:00 PM	
5:00 PM	
6:00 PM	
7:00 PM	
8:00 PM	
9:00 PM	
10:00 PM	
11:00 PM	

Tuesday

11/12/2019

Things to Accomplish

_____

_____

_____

_____

Writing Goals

_____

_____

_____

"Success is walking from
failure to failure with no loss
of enthusiasm."
—Winston Churchill

5:00 AM	
6:00 AM	
7:00 AM	
8:00 AM	
9:00 AM	
10:00 AM	
11:00 AM	
12:00 PM	
1:00 PM	
2:00 PM	
3:00 PM	
4:00 PM	
5:00 PM	
6:00 PM	
7:00 PM	
8:00 PM	
9:00 PM	
10:00 PM	
11:00 PM	

Wednesday
11/13/2019
Things to Accomplish

_____

_____

_____

_____

Writing Goals

_____

_____

_____

Limit your "always" and your
"nevers."
—Amy Poehler

5:00 AM	
6:00 AM	
7:00 AM	
8:00 AM	
9:00 AM	
10:00 AM	
11:00 AM	
12:00 PM	
1:00 PM	
2:00 PM	
3:00 PM	
4:00 PM	
5:00 PM	
6:00 PM	
7:00 PM	
8:00 PM	
9:00 PM	
10:00 PM	
11:00 PM	

Thursday
11/14/2019

Things to Accomplish

_____

_____

_____

_____

Writing Goals

_____

_____

_____

"If you are always trying to be
normal you will never know
how amazing you can be."
—Maya Angelou

5:00 AM	
6:00 AM	
7:00 AM	
8:00 AM	
9:00 AM	
10:00 AM	
1:00 AM	
12:00 PM	
1:00 PM	
2:00 PM	
3:00 PM	
4:00 PM	
5:00 PM	
6:00 PM	
7:00 PM	
8:00 PM	
9:00 PM	
10:00 PM	
11:00 PM	

Friday

11/15/2019

Things to Accomplish

_____

_____

_____

_____

Writing Goals

_____

_____

_____

"You make mistakes. Mistakes
don't make you."
—Maxwell Maltz

5:00 AM	
6:00 AM	
7:00 AM	
8:00 AM	
9:00 AM	
10:00 AM	
11:00 AM	
12:00 PM	
1:00 PM	
2:00 PM	
3:00 PM	
4:00 PM	
5:00 PM	
6:00 PM	
7:00 PM	
8:00 PM	
9:00 PM	
10:00 PM	
11:00 PM	

Saturday

11/16/2019

Things to Accomplish

_____

_____

_____

_____

Writing Goals

_____

_____

_____

"To begin, begin."
—William Wordsworth

5:00 AM	
6:00 AM	
7:00 AM	
8:00 AM	
9:00 AM	
10:00 AM	
11:00 AM	
12:00 PM	
1:00 PM	
2:00 PM	
3:00 PM	
4:00 PM	
5:00 PM	
6:00 PM	
7:00 PM	
8:00 PM	
9:00 PM	
10:00 PM	
11:00 PM	

Sunday

11/17/2019

Things to Accomplish

_____

_____

_____

_____

Writing Goals

_____

_____

_____

"Be so good they can't ignore you."
—Steve Martin

5:00 AM	
6:00 AM	
7:00 AM	
8:00 AM	
9:00 AM	
10:00 AM	
11:00 AM	
12:00 PM	
1:00 PM	
2:00 PM	
3:00 PM	
4:00 PM	
5:00 PM	
6:00 PM	
7:00 PM	
8:00 PM	
9:00 PM	
10:00 PM	
11:00 PM	

Weekly Planner

_____ to _____

Goals

_____

_____

_____

_____

_____

Notes

MONDAY _____

TUESDAY _____

WEDNESDAY _____

THURSDAY _____

FRIDAY _____

SATURDAY _____

SUNDAY _____

Monday

11/18/2019

Things to Accomplish

_____

_____

_____

_____

Writing Goals

_____

_____

_____

"Life is 10% what happens to you and 90% how you react to it."
—Charles R. Swindol

5:00 AM	
6:00 AM	
7:00 AM	
8:00 AM	
9:00 AM	
10:00 AM	
11:00 AM	
12:00 PM	
1:00 PM	
2:00 PM	
3:00 PM	
4:00 PM	
5:00 PM	
6:00 PM	
7:00 PM	
8:00 PM	
9:00 PM	
10:00 PM	
11:00 PM	

Tuesday

11/19/2019

Things to Accomplish

_____

_____

_____

_____

Writing Goals

_____

_____

_____

"The pessimist sees difficulty in every opportunity. The optimist sees opportunity in every difficulty."
—Winston Churchill

| 5:00 AM |
| 6:00 AM |
| 7:00 AM |
| 8:00 AM |
| 9:00 AM |
| 10:00 AM |
| 11:00 AM |
| 12:00 PM |
| 1:00 PM |
| 2:00 PM |
| 3:00 PM |
| 4:00 PM |
| 5:00 PM |
| 6:00 PM |
| 7:00 PM |
| 8:00 PM |
| 9:00 PM |
| 10:00 PM |
| 11:00 PM |

Wednesday

11/20/2019

Things to Accomplish

_____

_____

_____

_____

Writing Goals

_____

_____

_____

"Don't let yesterday take up
too much of today."
—Will Rogers

5:00 AM	
6:00 AM	
7:00 AM	
8:00 AM	
9:00 AM	
10:00 AM	
11:00 AM	
12:00 PM	
1:00 PM	
2:00 PM	
3:00 PM	
4:00 PM	
5:00 PM	
6:00 PM	
7:00 PM	
8:00 PM	
9:00 PM	
10:00 PM	
11:00 PM	

Thursday

11/21/2019

Things to Accomplish

_____

_____

_____

_____

Writing Goals

_____

_____

_____

"If you are working on
something that you really care
about, you don't have to be
pushed. The vision pulls
you."—Steve Jobs

5:00 AM	
6:00 AM	
7:00 AM	
8:00 AM	
9:00 AM	
10:00 AM	
11:00 AM	
12:00 PM	
1:00 PM	
2:00 PM	
3:00 PM	
4:00 PM	
5:00 PM	
6:00 PM	
7:00 PM	
8:00 PM	
9:00 PM	
10:00 PM	
11:00 PM	

Friday

11/22/2019

Things to Accomplish

_____

_____

_____

Writing Goals

_____

_____

_____

"People who are crazy enough
to think they can change the
world, are the ones who do."
—Rob Siltanen

5:00 AM	
6:00 AM	
7:00 AM	
8:00 AM	
9:00 AM	
10:00 AM	
11:00 AM	
12:00 PM	
1:00 PM	
2:00 PM	
3:00 PM	
4:00 PM	
5:00 PM	
6:00 PM	
7:00 PM	
8:00 PM	
9:00 PM	
10:00 PM	
11:00 PM	

Saturday

11/23/2019

Things to Accomplish

_____

_____

_____

_____

Writing Goals

_____

_____

_____

"Knowing is not enough; we must apply. Wishing is not enough; we must do."
—Johann Wolfgang von Goethe

5:00 AM	
6:00 AM	
7:00 AM	
8:00 AM	
9:00 AM	
10:00 AM	
11:00 AM	
12:00 PM	
1:00 PM	
2:00 PM	
3:00 PM	
4:00 PM	
5:00 PM	
6:00 PM	
7:00 PM	
8:00 PM	
9:00 PM	
10:00 PM	
11:00 PM	

Sunday
11/24/2019

Things to Accomplish

_____

_____

_____

Writing Goals

_____

_____

_____

"We generate fears while we sit. We overcome them by action."—Dr. Henry Link

5:00 AM	
6:00 AM	
7:00 AM	
8:00 AM	
9:00 AM	
10:00 AM	
11:00 AM	
12:00 PM	
1:00 PM	
2:00 PM	
3:00 PM	
4:00 PM	
5:00 PM	
6:00 PM	
7:00 PM	
8:00 PM	
9:00 PM	
10:00 PM	
11:00 PM	

Weekly Planner

_____ to _____

Goals

_____

_____

_____

_____

Notes

MONDAY _____

TUESDAY _____

WEDNESDAY _____

THURSDAY _____

FRIDAY _____

SATURDAY _____

SUNDAY _____

Monday
11/25/2019
Things to Accomplish

_____

_____

_____

_____

Writing Goals

_____

_____

_____

"The man who has confidence in himself gains the confidence of others."
—Hasidic proverb

5:00 AM	
6:00 AM	
7:00 AM	
8:00 AM	
9:00 AM	
10:00 AM	
11:00 AM	
12:00 PM	
1:00 PM	
2:00 PM	
3:00 PM	
4:00 PM	
5:00 PM	
6:00 PM	
7:00 PM	
8:00 PM	
9:00 PM	
10:00 PM	
11:00 PM	

Tuesday

11/26/2019

Things to Accomplish

_____

_____

_____

_____

Writing Goals

_____

_____

_____

"The only limit to our realization of tomorrow will be our doubts of today."
—Franklin D. Roosevelt

5:00 AM	
6:00 AM	
7:00 AM	
8:00 AM	
9:00 AM	
10:00 AM	
11:00 AM	
12:00 PM	
1:00 PM	
2:00 PM	
3:00 PM	
4:00 PM	
5:00 PM	
6:00 PM	
7:00 PM	
8:00 PM	
9:00 PM	
10:00 PM	
11:00 PM	

Wednesday

11/27/2019

Things to Accomplish

_____

_____

_____

_____

Writing Goals

_____

_____

_____

"Creativity is intelligence
having fun."
—Albert Einstein

5:00 AM	
6:00 AM	
7:00 AM	
8:00 AM	
9:00 AM	
10:00 AM	
11:00 AM	
12:00 PM	
1:00 PM	
2:00 PM	
3:00 PM	
4:00 PM	
5:00 PM	
6:00 PM	
7:00 PM	
8:00 PM	
9:00 PM	
10:00 PM	
11:00 PM	

Thursday

11/28/2019

Things to Accomplish

_____

_____

_____

_____

Writing Goals

_____

_____

_____

"What you lack in talent can be made up with desire, hustle and giving 110% all the time."—Don Zimmer

5:00 AM	
6:00 AM	
7:00 AM	
8:00 AM	
9:00 AM	
10:00 AM	
11:00 AM	
12:00 PM	
1:00 PM	
2:00 PM	
3:00 PM	
4:00 PM	
5:00 PM	
6:00 PM	
7:00 PM	
8:00 PM	
9:00 PM	
10:00 PM	
11:00 PM	

Friday

11/29/2019

Things to Accomplish

_____

_____

_____

_____

Writing Goals

_____

_____

_____

"Do what you can with all you
have, wherever you are."
—Theodore Roosevelt

5:00 AM	
6:00 AM	
7:00 AM	
8:00 AM	
9:00 AM	
10:00 AM	
11:00 AM	
12:00 PM	
1:00 PM	
2:00 PM	
3:00 PM	
4:00 PM	
5:00 PM	
6:00 PM	
7:00 PM	
8:00 PM	
9:00 PM	
10:00 PM	
11:00 PM	

Saturday

11/30/2019

Things to Accomplish

_____

_____

_____

Writing Goals

_____

_____

_____

"Reading is to the mind, as
exercise is to the body."
—Brian Tracy

5:00 AM	
6:00 AM	
7:00 AM	
8:00 AM	
9:00 AM	
10:00 AM	
11:00 AM	
12:00 PM	
1:00 PM	
2:00 PM	
3:00 PM	
4:00 PM	
5:00 PM	
6:00 PM	
7:00 PM	
8:00 PM	
9:00 PM	
10:00 PM	
11:00 PM	

Sunday

12/1/2019

Things to Accomplish

_____

_____

_____

_____

Writing Goals

_____

_____

_____

"For every reason it's not
possible, there are hundreds
of people who have faced the
same circumstances and
succeeded."—Jack Canfield

5:00 AM	
6:00 AM	
7:00 AM	
8:00 AM	
9:00 AM	
10:00 AM	
11:00 AM	
12:00 PM	
1:00 PM	
2:00 PM	
3:00 PM	
4:00 PM	
5:00 PM	
6:00 PM	
7:00 PM	
8:00 PM	
9:00 PM	
10:00 PM	
11:00 PM	

Weekly Planner

_____ to _____

Goals

_____

_____

_____

_____

_____

Notes

MONDAY _____

TUESDAY _____

WEDNESDAY _____

THURSDAY _____

FRIDAY _____

SATURDAY _____

SUNDAY _____

Monday

12/2/2019

Things to Accomplish

_____

_____

_____

_____

Writing Goals

_____

_____

_____

"Things work out best for
those who make the best of
how things work out."
—John Wooden

5:00 AM	
6:00 AM	
7:00 AM	
8:00 AM	
9:00 AM	
10:00 AM	
11:00 AM	
12:00 PM	
1:00 PM	
2:00 PM	
3:00 PM	
4:00 PM	
5:00 PM	
6:00 PM	
7:00 PM	
8:00 PM	
9:00 PM	
10:00 PM	
11:00 PM	

Tuesday
12/3/2019

Things to Accomplish

_____

_____

_____

_____

Writing Goals

_____

_____

_____

"I think goals should never be easy, they should force you to work, even if they are uncomfortable at the time."
—Michael Phelps

5:00 AM	
6:00 AM	
7:00 AM	
8:00 AM	
9:00 AM	
10:00 AM	
11:00 AM	
12:00 PM	
1:00 PM	
2:00 PM	
3:00 PM	
4:00 PM	
5:00 PM	
6:00 PM	
7:00 PM	
8:00 PM	
9:00 PM	
10:00 PM	
11:00 PM	

Wednesday

12/4/2019

Things to Accomplish

_____

_____

_____

_____

Writing Goals

_____

_____

_____

"Today's accomplishments
were yesterday's
impossibilities."
—Robert H. Schuller

| 5:00 AM |
| 6:00 AM |
| 7:00 AM |
| 8:00 AM |
| 9:00 AM |
| 10:00 AM |
| 11:00 AM |
| 12:00 PM |
| 1:00 PM |
| 2:00 PM |
| 3:00 PM |
| 4:00 PM |
| 5:00 PM |
| 6:00 PM |
| 7:00 PM |
| 8:00 PM |
| 9:00 PM |
| 10:00 PM |
| 11:00 PM |

Thursday

12/5/2019

Things to Accomplish

_____

_____

_____

_____

Writing Goals

_____

_____

_____

"You don't have to be great to start, but you have to start to be great."—Zig Ziglar

5:00 AM	
6:00 AM	
7:00 AM	
8:00 AM	
9:00 AM	
10:00 AM	
11:00 AM	
12:00 PM	
1:00 PM	
2:00 PM	
3:00 PM	
4:00 PM	
5:00 PM	
6:00 PM	
7:00 PM	
8:00 PM	
9:00 PM	
10:00 PM	
11:00 PM	

Friday

12/6/2019

Things to Accomplish

_____

_____

_____

_____

Writing Goals

_____

_____

_____

"Success is going from failure to failure without losing your enthusiasm."
—Winston Churchill

5:00 AM	
6:00 AM	
7:00 AM	
8:00 AM	
9:00 AM	
10:00 AM	
11:00 AM	
12:00 PM	
1:00 PM	
2:00 PM	
3:00 PM	
4:00 PM	
5:00 PM	
6:00 PM	
7:00 PM	
8:00 PM	
9:00 PM	
10:00 PM	
11:00 PM	

Saturday

12/7/2019

Things to Accomplish

_____

_____

_____

Writing Goals

_____

_____

_____

"Dream big and dare to fail."
—Norman Vaughan

5:00 AM	
6:00 AM	
7:00 AM	
8:00 AM	
9:00 AM	
10:00 AM	
11:00 AM	
12:00 PM	
1:00 PM	
2:00 PM	
3:00 PM	
4:00 PM	
5:00 PM	
6:00 PM	
7:00 PM	
8:00 PM	
9:00 PM	
10:00 PM	
11:00 PM	

Sunday

12/8/2019

Things to Accomplish

_____

_____

_____

_____

Writing Goals

_____

_____

_____

"Tough times never last, but
tough people do."
—Dr. Robert Schuller

5:00 AM	
6:00 AM	
7:00 AM	
8:00 AM	
9:00 AM	
10:00 AM	
11:00 AM	
12:00 PM	
1:00 PM	
2:00 PM	
3:00 PM	
4:00 PM	
5:00 PM	
6:00 PM	
7:00 PM	
8:00 PM	
9:00 PM	
10:00 PM	
11:00 PM	

Weekly Planner

_____ to _____

Goals

_____

_____

_____

_____

_____

Notes

MONDAY	_____

TUESDAY	_____

WEDNESDAY	_____

THURSDAY	_____

FRIDAY	_____

SATURDAY	_____

SUNDAY	_____

Monday

12/9/2019

Things to Accomplish

_____

_____

_____

_____

Writing Goals

_____

_____

_____

"The best way out is always through."—Robert Frost

5:00 AM	
6:00 AM	
7:00 AM	
8:00 AM	
9:00 AM	
10:00 AM	
11:00 AM	
12:00 PM	
1:00 PM	
2:00 PM	
3:00 PM	
4:00 PM	
5:00 PM	
6:00 PM	
7:00 PM	
8:00 PM	
9:00 PM	
10:00 PM	
11:00 PM	

Tuesday
12/10/2019

Things to Accomplish

_____

_____

_____

_____

Writing Goals

_____

_____

_____

"The difference between
ordinary and extraordinary is
that little extra."
—Jimmy Johnson

5:00 AM	
6:00 AM	
7:00 AM	
8:00 AM	
9:00 AM	
10:00 AM	
11:00 AM	
12:00 PM	
1:00 PM	
2:00 PM	
3:00 PM	
4:00 PM	
5:00 PM	
6:00 PM	
7:00 PM	
8:00 PM	
9:00 PM	
10:00 PM	
11:00 PM	

Wednesday

12/11/2019

Things to Accomplish

_____

_____

_____

_____

Writing Goals

_____

_____

_____

"You must not only aim right, but draw the bow with all your might."
—Henry David Thoreau

5:00 AM	
6:00 AM	
7:00 AM	
8:00 AM	
9:00 AM	
10:00 AM	
11:00 AM	
12:00 PM	
1:00 PM	
2:00 PM	
3:00 PM	
4:00 PM	
5:00 PM	
6:00 PM	
7:00 PM	
8:00 PM	
9:00 PM	
10:00 PM	
11:00 PM	

Thursday

12/12/2019

Things to Accomplish

_____

_____

_____

_____

Writing Goals

_____

_____

_____

"Even if you're on the right track, you'll get run over if you just sit there."—Will Rogers

5:00 AM	
6:00 AM	
7:00 AM	
8:00 AM	
9:00 AM	
10:00 AM	
1:00 AM	
12:00 PM	
1:00 PM	
2:00 PM	
3:00 PM	
4:00 PM	
5:00 PM	
6:00 PM	
7:00 PM	
8:00 PM	
9:00 PM	
10:00 PM	
11:00 PM	

Friday

12/13/2019

Things to Accomplish

_____

_____

_____

_____

Writing Goals

_____

_____

_____

"Everything you've ever wanted is on the other side of fear."—George Addair

5:00 AM	
6:00 AM	
7:00 AM	
8:00 AM	
9:00 AM	
10:00 AM	
11:00 AM	
12:00 PM	
1:00 PM	
2:00 PM	
3:00 PM	
4:00 PM	
5:00 PM	
6:00 PM	
7:00 PM	
8:00 PM	
9:00 PM	
10:00 PM	
11:00 PM	

Saturday

12/14/2019

Things to Accomplish

_____

_____

_____

_____

Writing Goals

_____

_____

_____

"A year from now you may
wish you had started today."
—Karen Lamb

5:00 AM	
6:00 AM	
7:00 AM	
8:00 AM	
9:00 AM	
10:00 AM	
11:00 AM	
12:00 PM	
1:00 PM	
2:00 PM	
3:00 PM	
4:00 PM	
5:00 PM	
6:00 PM	
7:00 PM	
8:00 PM	
9:00 PM	
10:00 PM	
11:00 PM	

Sunday

12/15/2019

Things to Accomplish

_____

_____

_____

_____

Writing Goals

_____

_____

_____

"To avoid criticism, do nothing, say nothing, be nothing."—Elbert Hubbard

5:00 AM	
6:00 AM	
7:00 AM	
8:00 AM	
9:00 AM	
10:00 AM	
11:00 AM	
12:00 PM	
1:00 PM	
2:00 PM	
3:00 PM	
4:00 PM	
5:00 PM	
6:00 PM	
7:00 PM	
8:00 PM	
9:00 PM	
10:00 PM	
11:00 PM	

Weekly Planner

_____ to _____

Goals

_____

_____

_____

_____

_____

Notes

MONDAY _____

TUESDAY _____

WEDNESDAY _____

THURSDAY _____

FRIDAY _____

SATURDAY _____

SUNDAY _____

Monday

12/16/2019

Things to Accomplish

_____

_____

_____

_____

Writing Goals

_____

_____

_____

"The dreamers are the saviors
of the world."
—James Allen

5:00 AM	
6:00 AM	
7:00 AM	
8:00 AM	
9:00 AM	
10:00 AM	
11:00 AM	
12:00 PM	
1:00 PM	
2:00 PM	
3:00 PM	
4:00 PM	
5:00 PM	
6:00 PM	
7:00 PM	
8:00 PM	
9:00 PM	
10:00 PM	
11:00 PM	

Tuesday

12/17/2019

Things to Accomplish

_____

_____

_____

_____

Writing Goals

_____

_____

_____

"If you aren't going all the
way, why go at all?"
—Joe Namath

5:00 AM	
6:00 AM	
7:00 AM	
8:00 AM	
9:00 AM	
10:00 AM	
11:00 AM	
12:00 PM	
1:00 PM	
2:00 PM	
3:00 PM	
4:00 PM	
5:00 PM	
6:00 PM	
7:00 PM	
8:00 PM	
9:00 PM	
10:00 PM	
11:00 PM	

Wednesday

12/18/2019

Things to Accomplish

_____

_____

_____

Writing Goals

_____

_____

_____

"Just keep going. Everybody
gets better if they keep at it."
—Ted Williams

5:00 AM	
6:00 AM	
7:00 AM	
8:00 AM	
9:00 AM	
10:00 AM	
11:00 AM	
12:00 PM	
1:00 PM	
2:00 PM	
3:00 PM	
4:00 PM	
5:00 PM	
6:00 PM	
7:00 PM	
8:00 PM	
9:00 PM	
10:00 PM	
11:00 PM	

Thursday

12/19/2019

Things to Accomplish

_____

_____

_____

_____

Writing Goals

_____

_____

_____

"You miss 100% of the shots
you don't take."
—Wayne Gretzky

5:00 AM	
6:00 AM	
7:00 AM	
8:00 AM	
9:00 AM	
10:00 AM	
11:00 AM	
12:00 PM	
1:00 PM	
2:00 PM	
3:00 PM	
4:00 PM	
5:00 PM	
6:00 PM	
7:00 PM	
8:00 PM	
9:00 PM	
10:00 PM	
11:00 PM	

Friday

12/20/2019

Things to Accomplish

_____

_____

_____

_____

Writing Goals

_____

_____

_____

Rewrite this opening scene to better connect readers to the character: Jr. sat beneath the ancient oak, loading rounds into his .12 Gauge shotgun, waiting for that thing to return. He pulled a Polaroid of his wife and two-year-old daughter from his back pocket. This ends tonight. —Ben Eads

5:00 AM	
6:00 AM	
7:00 AM	
8:00 AM	
9:00 AM	
10:00 AM	
11:00 AM	
12:00 PM	
1:00 PM	
2:00 PM	
3:00 PM	
4:00 PM	
5:00 PM	
6:00 PM	
7:00 PM	
8:00 PM	
9:00 PM	
10:00 PM	
11:00 PM	

Saturday

12/21/2019

Things to Accomplish

_____

_____

_____

Writing Goals

_____

_____

_____

"Never let your memories be
greater than your dreams."
—Doug Ivester

5:00 AM	
6:00 AM	
7:00 AM	
8:00 AM	
9:00 AM	
10:00 AM	
11:00 AM	
12:00 PM	
1:00 PM	
2:00 PM	
3:00 PM	
4:00 PM	
5:00 PM	
6:00 PM	
7:00 PM	
8:00 PM	
9:00 PM	
10:00 PM	
11:00 PM	

Sunday

12/22/2019

Things to Accomplish

_____

_____

_____

_____

Writing Goals

_____

_____

_____

Our greatest glory is not in
never falling, but in rising
every time we fall.
—Confucius

5:00 AM	
6:00 AM	
7:00 AM	
8:00 AM	
9:00 AM	
10:00 AM	
11:00 AM	
12:00 PM	
1:00 PM	
2:00 PM	
3:00 PM	
4:00 PM	
5:00 PM	
6:00 PM	
7:00 PM	
8:00 PM	
9:00 PM	
10:00 PM	
11:00 PM	

Struggling to finish that first draft?
Unsure about your options for publication?
Need to figure out how to market your book?

We know exactly how you feel because we have been there too.
You can benefit from our years of experience as multi-genre
authors. We do not teach you how to write – it is our mission to
provide you with the tools to become a successful authorpreneur.

Our services include:

- *Kick the Muse to the Curb* Finishing School
- Live training courses via Skype
- Coaching to help you achieve your creative goals
- Editing of fiction and non-fiction
- Proofreading of fiction and non-fiction
- Indexing of non-fiction books
- Illustration of children's books
- Author photographs
- Non-stock professional photographs
- Publication services (e-book and paperback)

Dreams
to Realities

Goals into
Achievements

Inspiration
to Results

We also understand about budgets, so contact us for a quotation
and tell us how we can help you make your dream a reality.

Muses & Broomsticks

Email: muses.brooms@gmail.com
WhatsApp message: **+27 (0)60 896 1746**
Facebook: **@MusesAndBroomsticks**
Website/blog: **www.MusesAndBroomsticks.com**

Company Reg No. 2015/071485/07 Not registered for VAT

More titles from Crystal Lake Publishing

Tales from the Darkest Depths

Weekly Planner

_____ to _____

Goals

_____

_____

_____

_____

_____

Notes

MONDAY _____

TUESDAY _____

WEDNESDAY _____

THURSDAY _____

FRIDAY _____

SATURDAY _____

SUNDAY _____

Monday
12/23/2019

Things to Accomplish

_____

_____

_____

_____

Writing Goals

_____

_____

_____

Hardships often prepare
ordinary people for an
extraordinary destiny.
—C.S. Lewis

| 5:00 AM |
| 6:00 AM |
| 7:00 AM |
| 8:00 AM |
| 9:00 AM |
| 10:00 AM |
| 11:00 AM |
| 12:00 PM |
| 1:00 PM |
| 2:00 PM |
| 3:00 PM |
| 4:00 PM |
| 5:00 PM |
| 6:00 PM |
| 7:00 PM |
| 8:00 PM |
| 9:00 PM |
| 10:00 PM |
| 11:00 PM |

Tuesday

12/24/2019

Things to Accomplish

_____

_____

_____

_____

Writing Goals

_____

_____

_____

Believe in yourself. You are braver than you think, more talented than you know, and capable of more than you imagine.
—Roy T. Bennett

5:00 AM	
6:00 AM	
7:00 AM	
8:00 AM	
9:00 AM	
10:00 AM	
11:00 AM	
12:00 PM	
1:00 PM	
2:00 PM	
3:00 PM	
4:00 PM	
5:00 PM	
6:00 PM	
7:00 PM	
8:00 PM	
9:00 PM	
10:00 PM	
11:00 PM	

Wednesday

12/25/2019

Things to Accomplish

_____

_____

_____

_____

Writing Goals

_____

_____

_____

A goal is not always meant to be reached, it often serves simply as something to aim at. —Bruce Lee

5:00 AM	
6:00 AM	
7:00 AM	
8:00 AM	
9:00 AM	
10:00 AM	
11:00 AM	
12:00 PM	
1:00 PM	
2:00 PM	
3:00 PM	
4:00 PM	
5:00 PM	
6:00 PM	
7:00 PM	
8:00 PM	
9:00 PM	
10:00 PM	
11:00 PM	

Thursday

12/26/2019

Things to Accomplish

_____

_____

_____

_____

Writing Goals

_____

_____

_____

Your true success in life begins
only when you make the
commitment to become
excellent at what you do.
—Brian Tracy

5:00 AM	
6:00 AM	
7:00 AM	
8:00 AM	
9:00 AM	
10:00 AM	
11:00 AM	
12:00 PM	
1:00 PM	
2:00 PM	
3:00 PM	
4:00 PM	
5:00 PM	
6:00 PM	
7:00 PM	
8:00 PM	
9:00 PM	
10:00 PM	
11:00 PM	

Friday

12/27/2019

Things to Accomplish

_____

_____

_____

_____

Writing Goals

_____

_____

_____

Definiteness of purpose is the
starting point of all
achievement.
—W. Clement Stone

5:00 AM	
6:00 AM	
7:00 AM	
8:00 AM	
9:00 AM	
10:00 AM	
11:00 AM	
12:00 PM	
1:00 PM	
2:00 PM	
3:00 PM	
4:00 PM	
5:00 PM	
6:00 PM	
7:00 PM	
8:00 PM	
9:00 PM	
10:00 PM	
11:00 PM	

Saturday

12/28/2019

Things to Accomplish

_____

_____

_____

_____

Writing Goals

_____

_____

_____

Too many of us are not living
our dreams because we are
living our fears.—Les Brown

5:00 AM	
6:00 AM	
7:00 AM	
8:00 AM	
9:00 AM	
10:00 AM	
1:00 AM	
12:00 PM	
1:00 PM	
2:00 PM	
3:00 PM	
4:00 PM	
5:00 PM	
6:00 PM	
7:00 PM	
8:00 PM	
9:00 PM	
10:00 PM	
11:00 PM	

Sunday
12/29/2019
Things to Accomplish

_____

_____

_____

_____

Writing Goals

_____

_____

_____

Hard times don't create heroes. It is during the hard times when the 'hero' within us is revealed.—Bob Riley

5:00 AM	
6:00 AM	
7:00 AM	
8:00 AM	
9:00 AM	
10:00 AM	
11:00 AM	
12:00 PM	
1:00 PM	
2:00 PM	
3:00 PM	
4:00 PM	
5:00 PM	
6:00 PM	
7:00 PM	
8:00 PM	
9:00 PM	
10:00 PM	
11:00 PM	

Weekly Planner

_____ to _____

Goals

_____

_____

_____

_____

_____

Notes

MONDAY   _____

TUESDAY   _____

WEDNESDAY   _____

THURSDAY   _____

FRIDAY   _____

SATURDAY   _____

SUNDAY   _____

Monday
12/30/2019

Things to Accomplish

_____

_____

_____

_____

Writing Goals

_____

_____

_____

Start by doing what's
necessary; then do what's
possible; and suddenly you
are doing the impossible.
—Francis of Assisi

| 5:00 AM |
| 6:00 AM |
| 7:00 AM |
| 8:00 AM |
| 9:00 AM |
| 10:00 AM |
| 11:00 AM |
| 12:00 PM |
| 1:00 PM |
| 2:00 PM |
| 3:00 PM |
| 4:00 PM |
| 5:00 PM |
| 6:00 PM |
| 7:00 PM |
| 8:00 PM |
| 9:00 PM |
| 10:00 PM |
| 11:00 PM |

Tuesday

12/31/2019

Things to Accomplish

_____

_____

_____

_____

Writing Goals

_____

_____

_____

I am not a product of my
circumstances. I am a product
of my decisions.
—Stephen Covey

5:00 AM	
6:00 AM	
7:00 AM	
8:00 AM	
9:00 AM	
10:00 AM	
11:00 AM	
12:00 PM	
1:00 PM	
2:00 PM	
3:00 PM	
4:00 PM	
5:00 PM	
6:00 PM	
7:00 PM	
8:00 PM	
9:00 PM	
10:00 PM	
11:00 PM	

Wednesday

1/1/2020

Things to Accomplish

_____

_____

_____

_____

Writing Goals

_____

_____

_____

Twenty years from now you will be more disappointed by the things you didn't do than by the things you did.
—Mark Twain

5:00 AM	
6:00 AM	
7:00 AM	
8:00 AM	
9:00 AM	
10:00 AM	
11:00 AM	
12:00 PM	
1:00 PM	
2:00 PM	
3:00 PM	
4:00 PM	
5:00 PM	
6:00 PM	
7:00 PM	
8:00 PM	
9:00 PM	
10:00 PM	
11:00 PM	

Thursday

1/2/2020

Things to Accomplish

_____

_____

_____

_____

Writing Goals

_____

_____

_____

A goal is a dream with a
deadline.—Napoleon Hill

| 5:00 AM |
| 6:00 AM |
| 7:00 AM |
| 8:00 AM |
| 9:00 AM |
| 10:00 AM |
| 11:00 AM |
| 12:00 PM |
| 1:00 PM |
| 2:00 PM |
| 3:00 PM |
| 4:00 PM |
| 5:00 PM |
| 6:00 PM |
| 7:00 PM |
| 8:00 PM |
| 9:00 PM |
| 10:00 PM |
| 11:00 PM |

Friday

1/3/2020

Things to Accomplish

_____

_____

_____

_____

Writing Goals

_____

_____

_____

Your mind is a powerful thing.
When you fill it with positive
thoughts, your life will start to
change— Unknown

5:00 AM	
6:00 AM	
7:00 AM	
8:00 AM	
9:00 AM	
10:00 AM	
11:00 AM	
12:00 PM	
1:00 PM	
2:00 PM	
3:00 PM	
4:00 PM	
5:00 PM	
6:00 PM	
7:00 PM	
8:00 PM	
9:00 PM	
10:00 PM	
11:00 PM	

Saturday

1/4/2020

Things to Accomplish

_____

_____

_____

_____

Writing Goals

_____

_____

_____

We are all apprentices in a
craft where no one ever
becomes a master.
—Ernest Hemingway

5:00 AM	
6:00 AM	
7:00 AM	
8:00 AM	
9:00 AM	
10:00 AM	
11:00 AM	
12:00 PM	
1:00 PM	
2:00 PM	
3:00 PM	
4:00 PM	
5:00 PM	
6:00 PM	
7:00 PM	
8:00 PM	
9:00 PM	
10:00 PM	
11:00 PM	

Sunday
1/5/2020

Things to Accomplish

_____

_____

_____

_____

Writing Goals

_____

_____

_____

"It always seems impossible
until it's done."
—Nelson Mandela

5:00 AM	
6:00 AM	
7:00 AM	
8:00 AM	
9:00 AM	
10:00 AM	
11:00 AM	
12:00 PM	
1:00 PM	
2:00 PM	
3:00 PM	
4:00 PM	
5:00 PM	
6:00 PM	
7:00 PM	
8:00 PM	
9:00 PM	
10:00 PM	
11:00 PM	

You're Beautiful

You're beautiful
Don't let anyone tell you otherwise.
If someone calls you ugly, fat, stupid, pointless or nothing; don't
    listen.
Don't call it them back.
If you use those words about others or yourself, you give them
    permission to use those words too.
Instead, look at the mirror in front of you and inside you.
See how special you are.
See the real you—how unique and beautiful you are.
Open your eyes, and acknowledge yourself,
And your beauty.
You matter.

—Theresa Derwin

CRYSTAL LAKE'S

AUTHOR CENTRAL

LET US BE YOUR GUIDE

Check out our Author Central page
for mentoring packages, editing
services, author workshops, and
other recommended services.

Thanks to all the authors who contributed quotes and exercises, as well as wisdomquotes.com, Writers Digest, quotes.com, and Brainy Quote.